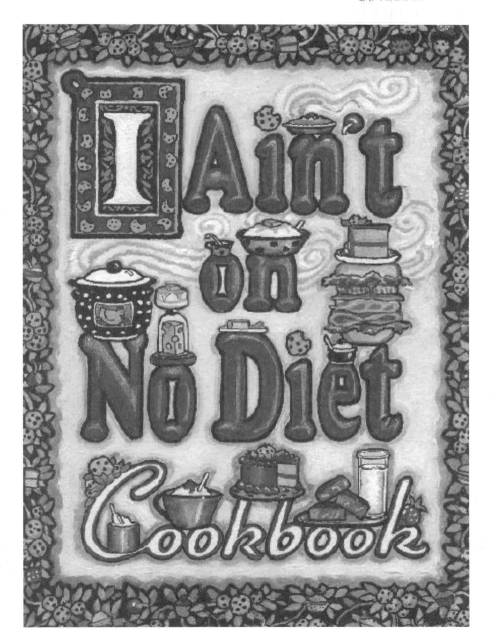

I Ain't on No Diet Cookbook

1st Printing June 2005

ISBN 1-931294-93-3

Library of Congress Number: 2005927195

Edited, Designed and Published in the
United States of America and
Manufactured in China by
Cookbook Resources, LLC
541 Doubletree Drive
Highland Village, Texas 75077
Toll free 866-229-2665
www.cookbookresources.com

Introduction

There are diets, diets and more diets. We're constantly bombarded with low calorie, fat–free and weight–reducing media. Ah, and the controversy surrounding all these topics sends us all into a tailspin. I think you know what I mean. Whew! The diet madness just makes me even hungrier.

This book is about breaking the diet cycle and being happy with cooking and eating the foods we love. Stop starving yourself! It's okay to moderately indulge in wholesome, real food that is simple to prepare, tastes good and makes us happy. Just be sensible.

The recipes in the **I Ain't on No Diet Cookbook** use real cheese, cream, sugar, butter, eggs and other deliciously "forbidden" ingredients, and they are fabulous.

If you're craving some good, down-home eating, I know you'll love these favorites:

- **Incredible Broccoli-Cheese Soup**
- **Santa Fe Stew**
- **Easy-Going Hot Bunwiches**
- **Quick Broccoli-Noodle Salad**
- **Extreme Cheddar-Potato Casserole**
- **Fettuccine Supreme**
- **Mom's Best Pot Roast**
- **Speedy Chicken and Tortilla Dumplings**
- **Southern Pecan Pie**
- **Great Coconut-Cake Deluxe**
- **Macadamia Nut Cookies**

You, your family and friends will savor the many delicious dishes within this book. Of course, moderation is always the key, but don't let that stop you or your loved ones from enjoying food!

The **I Ain't on No Diet Cookbook**, well, it's for the joy of food and for the love of family. Now, let's eat!

CONTENTS

CONTENTS

Appetizers
& Beverages

Baked Asparagus Tidbits

20 thin slices white bread
1 (8 ounce) package cream cheese, softened
3 tablespoons butter, softened
1 egg
½ teaspoon seasoned salt
20 canned asparagus spears, drained
¾ cup (1½ sticks) butter, melted

Preheat oven to 400°. Remove crusts from bread and flatten slices with rolling pin. In mixing bowl combine cream cheese, butter, egg and seasoned salt. Spread mixture evenly over bread slices.

Place an asparagus spear on each one and roll up. Dip in melted butter to coat all sides. Place on baking sheet and freeze until ready to bake. Cut frozen rolls into thirds and bake for 15 minutes or until light brown. Serve immediately.

Spiced Pecans to Love

These will disappear! My friend made these for everybody in the bridge club – now we expect them every year.

2 cups sugar
½ cup water
2 teaspoons cinnamon
¼ teaspoon salt
1 teaspoon ground nutmeg
½ teaspoon ground cloves
4 cups pecan halves

Combine all ingredients except pecans in deep dish and mix well. Cover mixture with wax paper and microwave on HIGH for 4 minutes.

(Continued on next page.)

(Continued)

Stir and microwave for another 4 minutes. Add pecans and quickly mix well. Spread on wax paper to cool. Break apart and store in covered container.

Cheesy Spinach Bites

¼ cup (½ stick) butter
1 cup flour
3 eggs
1 cup milk
1 teaspoon salt
1 teaspoon baking powder
1 teaspoon dry mustard
1 (10 ounce) package frozen spinach, thawed, drained, squeezed dry
1 (8 ounce) package shredded mozzarella cheese
1 (8 ounce) package shredded cheddar cheese

Preheat oven to 350°. Melt butter in 9 x 13-inch baking dish in oven.

In large mixing bowl, combine flour, eggs, milk, salt, baking powder and mustard and mix well. Add spinach and cheese, pour into pan and bake for 30 minutes.

When set, cut into squares and serve warm. Recipe may be reheated.

Great Olive Puffs

2 cups shredded, sharp cheddar cheese
½ cup (1 stick) butter, very soft
½ teaspoon salt
1 teaspoon paprika
½ teaspoon garlic powder
1 cup flour
48 green stuffed olives

Preheat oven to 375°. In large mixing bowl, combine cheese and butter. Stir in dry ingredients and mix well.

Wrap teaspoon of mixture around each olive and place on baking sheet. Bake for 15 to 16 minutes.

Corny Walnut Dip
Try this one – you'll love it!

2 (8 ounce) packages cream cheese, softened
¼ cup lime juice
1 tablespoon cumin
1 teaspoon salt
1 teaspoon cayenne pepper
1 (8 ounce) can whole kernel corn, drained
1 cup chopped walnuts
1 (4 ounce) can chopped green chilies, drained
3 green onions and tops, chopped

In mixing bowl, whip cream cheese until fluffy. Beat in lime juice, cumin, salt and cayenne pepper. Stir in corn, walnuts, green chilies and onions.

Chill before serving. Serve with tortilla chips.

Supreme Nachos Supreme
Different but people like the change.

1 tablespoon oil
⅓ cup finely diced bell pepper
½ cup finely diced onion
⅔ cup fresh whole kernel corn
1 (4 ounce) can chopped green chilies, drained
1 (8 ounce) package cream cheese, softened
1 teaspoon chili powder
1 teaspoon ground cumin
⅛ teaspoon cayenne pepper (optional)
½ teaspoon salt
2 cups grated Monterey Jack cheese
Tortilla chips
Thinly sliced jalapeno peppers

In large skillet, heat oil and lightly saute bell pepper, onion and corn. Stir in green chilies.

In medium mixing bowl, beat sour cream, cream cheese, chili powder, cumin, cayenne pepper and salt. Fold mixture into sautéed vegetables.

Place tortilla chips on baking sheet and spread vegetable mixture over top. Sprinkle Monterey Jack cheese and place 1 slice jalapeno pepper over top of cheese. Broil for 2 to 3 minutes or until cheese melts.

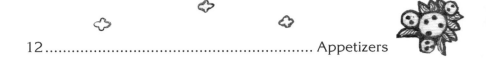

Pecan-Oat Munchies
This is great munching!

1 (16 ounce) package Quaker Oat Squares cereal
2 cups whole pecans
½ cup corn syrup
½ cup packed brown sugar
¼ cup (½ stick) butter
1 teaspoon vanilla
½ teaspoon baking soda

Preheat oven to 250°. Combine cereal and pecans in
9 x 13-inch baking pan and set aside.

In 2-cup bowl, combine corn syrup, brown sugar and
butter. Microwave on HIGH for 1 minute, stir and turn
bowl. Microwave on HIGH again for 1 minute or until
mixture boils. Stir in vanilla and soda.

Pour mixture over cereal mixture and stir well to coat
evenly. Bake in oven for 1 hour and stir every 20 minutes.
Spread on baking sheet to cool.

Tropical Sausage Bites

1 pound cooked link sausage
1 pound hot bulk sausage
1 (8 ounce) can crushed pineapple with juice
1 cup apricot preserves
1 cup packed brown sugar
1 tablespoon white wine Worcestershire sauce

Slice link sausage into ¼-inch pieces. Shape bulk sausage into 1-inch balls and brown in skillet.

In separate large saucepan, combine pineapple, preserves, brown sugar and white wine Worcestershire sauce. Add sausages and simmer for 30 minutes.

Serve in chafing dish with cocktail picks.

Tasty Shrimp Dip

3 cups cooked, deveined shrimp, finely chopped
2 tablespoons horseradish
¼ cup chili sauce
⅔ cup mayonnaise
½ teaspoon salt
½ teaspoon white pepper

Combine all ingredients, mix well and chill. Serve with cucumber or zucchini slices.

Tip: If shrimp have been frozen, be sure to drain well.

Seafood Claws

1 (8 ounce) package cream cheese, softened
⅓ cup mayonnaise
⅓ cup sour cream
3 hard-boiled eggs, mashed
1 (8 ounce) can crabmeat, flaked
1 (8 ounce) can thinly cut shrimp, drained, chopped
¼ onion, very finely chopped
1 rib celery, very finely chopped
1 teaspoon Creole seasoning
Several dashes hot sauce

Combine cream cheese, mayonnaise, sour cream and boiled eggs in mixing bowl. Beat until fairly smooth.

Add crabmeat, shrimp, onion, celery, Creole seasoning and hot sauce and mix well.

Tip: This recipe can also be used as a dip or to make good sandwiches.

Irish Party Punch

This punch would also be a good one to use when the party is close to St. Patrick's Day!

1 (3 ounce) package lime gelatin
1 cup boiling water
1 (6 ounce) can frozen limeade
1 (6 ounce) can frozen lemonade
1 quart orange juice
1 quart pineapple juice
1 tablespoon almond extract
2 to 3 drops green food coloring
1 liter ginger ale, chilled

Dissolve lime gelatin in boiling water and stir well.

In gallon bottle, combine dissolved gelatin, limeade, lemonade, orange juice, pineapple juice, almond extract and food coloring. Chill. When ready to serve, add ginger ale. Serves 32.

Fantastic Coffee Punch

I promise that this will make a hit. Everyone will be back for seconds!

1 (2 ounce) jar instant coffee
2 quarts hot water
2¼ cups sugar
2 quarts half-and-half cream
1 quart ginger ale
1 pint heavy cream, whipped
½ gallon French vanilla ice cream

Dissolve instant coffee in hot water. When cool, add sugar and half-and-half cream and mix well. Chill.

When ready to serve, pour coffee-sugar mixture in punch bowl, add chilled ginger ale, whipped cream and ice cream. Let some chunks of ice cream remain. This will make 60 (4-ounce) servings.

Ruby Red Punch
The cranapple juice in this punch really makes it a "Christmas" special!

2 (6 ounce) cans frozen orange juice concentrate
4 cups water
2 (46 ounce) cans red Hawaiian punch
1 (46 ounce) can pineapple juice
1 (48 ounce) bottle cranapple juice
2 liters ginger ale, chilled

In 2 (1-gallon) bottles, combine orange juice, water, Hawaiian punch, pineapple juice and cranapple juice and stir well. Chill.

Place in punch bowl. Just before serving, add ginger ale. Makes 2 gallons.

Homemade Kahula

3 cups hot water
1 cup instant coffee granules
4 cups sugar
1 quart vodka
1 vanilla bean, split

In large saucepan, combine hot water and coffee and mix well. Add sugar and bring to boil for 2 minutes. Turn off heat and cool. Add vodka and vanilla bean.

Pour into bottle or jar and set for 30 days before serving. Shake occasionally.

Tip: If you happen to have some of the Mexican vanilla, you can make "instant" Kahula by using 3 tablespoons of Mexican vanilla instead of the vanilla bean, then you do not have to wait 30 days.

Breads
& Brunch

Crunchy Sticks

These are like breadsticks without going to the trouble of using yeast.
Good with pasta or salads too!

2 cups buttermilk baking mix
1 tablespoon dried onion flakes
1 egg
⅓ to ½ cup milk
½ cup (1 stick) butter
2 tablespoons dried parsley flakes
1½ teaspoon Italian herb seasoning
½ teaspoon paprika
⅓ cup grated parmesan cheese (optional)

Preheat oven to 375°. Combine mix, onion flakes, egg and just enough milk to make thick dough. Turn dough out on lightly floured surface and knead lightly. Pat into rectangle shape (about 9 x 13-inch).

Add butter to 10 x 14-inch pan and melt in hot oven. Cut dough into 12 or 14 strips with sharp knife or pizza cutter. Cut each strip in half and place evenly on top of melted butter in pan.

Combine parsley flakes, Italian seasoning, paprika and parmesan cheese and sprinkle mixture over strips. Bake for 10 to 12 minutes or until golden brown. Serve hot.

Tip: You can make them ahead of time if you need to, then reheat.

French Bread Monterey

1 loaf French bread, sliced
Butter, softened
1 cup mayonnaise
½ cup grated parmesan cheese
½ onion, finely chopped
½ teaspoon Worcestershire sauce
Paprika

Preheat oven to 200°. Spread bread slices completely with butter and place on baking sheet. Combine mayonnaise, cheese, onion and Worcestershire sauce.

Spread mixture on buttered bread and then sprinkle with paprika. Place bread in oven for 15 minutes then turn on broiler and brown lightly. Serve immediately.

Light and Crispy Waffles

2 cups biscuit mix
1 egg
½ cup oil
1⅓ cups club soda

Preheat waffle iron. In medium mixing bowl, combine all ingredients and stir by hand.

Pour just enough batter to cover waffle iron. Bake at 350° for about 10 minutes.

Tip: To have waffles for a "company weekend", make up all waffles; otherwise, freeze separately on baking sheet and place in large resealable storage bags. This recipe's batter can also be used for pancakes.

Merry Berry Strawberry Bread
Wonderful toasted for breakfast!

3 cups flour
2 cups sugar
1 teaspoon salt
1 teaspoon baking soda
2 teaspoons cinnamon
3 large eggs, beaten
1 cup oil
1¼ cups chopped pecans
2 (10 ounce) packages frozen sweetened strawberries,
  with juice

Preheat oven to 325°. Combine flour, sugar, salt, baking
soda and cinnamon into large mixing bowl. Add eggs and
oil and mix thoroughly. Fold in pecans and strawberries
and mix well.

Pour into 2 sprayed (5 x 9-inch) loaf pans and bake for
1 hour, 10 minutes. Test with toothpick to make sure
bread is done. Cool several minutes before removing from
pan.

Crunchy Bread Sticks

You won't believe how good these are and easy too!

1 (8 count) package hot dog buns
1 cup (2 sticks) butter, melted
Garlic powder
Paprika
Parmesan cheese

Preheat oven to 225°. Take each half bun and slice in half lengthwise.

Using pastry brush, butter all bread sticks and sprinkle light amount of garlic powder and just a few sprinkles of paprika and parmesan cheese. Place bread on baking sheet and bake for 45 minutes.

Tip: *It is good to have these made up and frozen because then you can take out just the number you want and warm them up.*

Grand Ginger Muffins

¾ cup (1½ sticks) butter, softened
¾ cup sugar
¼ cup corn syrup
¼ cup sorghum molasses
2 eggs
1 teaspoon baking soda
½ cup buttermilk
2 cups flour
Pinch of salt
1 teaspoon ground ginger
¼ teaspoon cinnamon
¼ cup raisins, optional
½ cup chopped pecans

Preheat oven to 350°. In mixing bowl, combine butter, sugar, syrup and molasses and mix well. Add eggs and beat well.

Stir baking soda into buttermilk, add to butter-sugar mixture and beat. Add flour, salt, ginger and cinnamon and beat. Stir in raisins and pecans and mix well.

Pour into 20 to 24 greased muffin tins and bake for 16 to 18 minutes or more depending on size of muffins.

Hidden Secret Muffins

When people taste these muffins, someone always says, "Yum. These are so good. What's in them?" And you'll say, "It's a secret."

Filling:

1 (8 ounce) package cream cheese, softened
1 egg
⅓ cup sugar
1 tablespoon grated orange rind

Muffin:

1 cup (2 sticks) butter, softened
1¾ cups sugar
3 eggs
3 cups flour
2 teaspoons baking powder
1 cup milk
1 teaspoon almond extract
1 cup chopped almonds, toasted

Preheat oven to 375°. To prepare filling, beat cream cheese, eggs, sugar and orange rind and set aside.

To prepare batter, cream butter and sugar until light and fluffy. Add eggs one at a time and beat after each addition.

Mix flour and baking powder and add alternately with milk to butter-sugar mixture. Begin and end with flour. Add almond extract and fold in almonds.

Fill 26 lightly greased muffin tins half full with batter. Spoon 1 heaping tablespoon filling in each muffin tin and top with muffin batter. Bake muffins for 20 to 25 minutes or until muffin bounces back when pressed or until they are light brown.

Maple-Spice Muffins

1 ¼ cups flour
1 ½ cups whole-wheat flour
½ cup quick-cooking oats
1 teaspoon baking soda
2 teaspoons baking powder
2 teaspoons cinnamon
½ teaspoon ground cloves
2 eggs
1 (8 ounce) carton sour cream
1 cup maple syrup
1 cup packed brown sugar
½ cup oil
½ teaspoon maple flavoring, optional
1 banana, mashed
1 cup chopped walnuts

Preheat oven to 375°. In mixing bowl, combine flours, oats, baking soda, baking powder, cinnamon and cloves and mix. Add eggs, sour cream, maple syrup, brown sugar, oil, maple flavoring and mashed banana. Stir well by hand.

Add walnuts and pour into 24 paper-lined muffin tins. Bake for 18 to 20 minutes.

Farmers' Breakfast Bake

1 pound hot sausage, cooked, crumbled
2 tablespoons dried onion flakes
1 (8 ounce) package grated cheddar cheese
1 cup biscuit mix
¼ teaspoon salt
¼ teaspoon pepper
5 eggs
2 cups milk

Preheat oven to 350°. Place cooked and crumbled sausage in sprayed 9 x 13-inch glass baking dish. Sprinkle with onion flakes and cheese.

In mixing bowl, combine biscuit mix, salt, pepper and eggs and beat well. Add milk, stir until fairly smooth and pour over sausage mixture. Bake for 35 minutes.

If you desire, prepare a day ahead, refrigerate and cook the following morning. Add 5 more minutes to cooking time if recipe is refrigerated. Serves 8.

Tip: For brunch, add 1 (8 ounce) can whole corn, drained.

Drum-Roll Green Chili Puff

This recipe is so versatile! Cut it in little squares and serve warm as an appetizer, for a brunch or for lunch. It would also go well with a Mexican meal – morning, noon or night!

10 eggs
½ cup flour
1 teaspoon baking powder
½ teaspoon salt
1 (16 ounce) carton small-curd cottage cheese
1 (8 ounce) package shredded mozzarella cheese
1 bunch green onions with tops, chopped
1 (8 ounce) package shredded cheddar cheese
½ cup (1 stick) butter, melted
1 (7 ounce) can chopped green chilies

Preheat oven to 350°. Beat eggs until light and lemon-colored. Add flour, baking powder and salt and beat until smooth. Add cottage cheese, mozzarella cheese, green onions, cheddar cheese, butter and green chilies. Mix well.

Pour mixture into sprayed 9 x 13-inch baking pan and bake for 40 minutes or until top is slightly brown around edges and center appears firm.

Serve immediately with salsa on the side.

Irresistible Quesadilla Pie

1 (4 ounce) can chopped green chilies, drained
½ pound sausage, cooked
1 (16 ounce) package grated cheddar cheese
3 eggs, well beaten
1½ cups milk
¾ cup biscuit mix
Hot salsa

Preheat oven to 350°. Spray 9-inch pie pan with non-stick cooking spray. Sprinkle green chilies, cooked sausage and cheddar cheese in pie pan.

In separate bowl, combine eggs, milk and biscuit mix. Pour mixture over chilies, sausage and cheese and bake for 30 to 40 minutes. Serve with salsa on top of each slice.

Glorious Pineapple-Cheese Casserole

This would be good served at a brunch or luncheon or as a side dish to sandwiches or ham. It's also great served at a morning bridge club along with coffee cake or delicious strawberry spread.

2 (20 ounce) cans pineapple chunks, drained
1 cup sugar
5 tablespoons flour
1½ cups grated cheddar cheese
1 stack round, buttery crackers, crushed
½ cup (1 stick) butter, melted

Preheat oven to 350°. Grease 9 x 13-inch baking dish and layer ingredients as follows: pineapple, sugar-flour mixture, cheese, cracker crumbs and butter drizzled over casserole.

Bake for 25 minutes or until bubbly.

Sausage-Chile Quiche

1 (9-inch) unbaked piecrust
1 (7 ounce) can whole green chilies, drained
1 pound hot sausage, cooked, crumbled, drained
4 eggs, slightly beaten
2 cups half-and-half cream
½ cup grated parmesan cheese
¾ cup grated Swiss cheese
½ teaspoon salt
¼ teaspoon pepper

Preheat oven to 350°. Line bottom of piecrust with split, seeded green chilies. Sprinkle sausage over chilies. Combine eggs, half-and-half cream, cheeses, salt and pepper and pour over sausage.

Cover edge of pastry with foil to prevent excessive browning. Bake for 35 minutes or until top is golden brown. Set aside quiche for about 5 minutes before serving.

Soups,
Sandwiches
& Salads

Incredible Broccoli-Cheese Soup

This really is an incredible soup!

1 (10 ounce) package frozen chopped broccoli
3 tablespoons butter
¼ onion, finely chopped
¼ cup flour
1 (16 ounce) carton half-and-half cream
1 (14 ounce) can chicken broth
½ teaspoon salt
¼ teaspoon black pepper
⅛ teaspoon cayenne pepper
½ teaspoon summer savory
1 (8 ounce) package mild Mexican-style cubed,
   processed cheese

Punch several holes in broccoli package and microwave
for 5 minutes. Turn package in microwave and cook
another 4 minutes. Leave in microwave for 3 minutes.

In large saucepan, melt butter and saute onion but do not
brown. Add flour, stir and gradually add half-and-half
cream, chicken broth and seasonings. Stir constantly and
heat until mixture is slightly thick. Do NOT let mixture
come to a boil.

Add cheese, stir and heat until cheese melts. Add cooked
broccoli. Serve piping hot. Serves 4 to 6.

Ultimate Cheddar Cheese Soup

1 cup finely chopped onion
1 red bell pepper, diced
2 tablespoons (¼ stick) butter
1 pound extra sharp cheddar cheese, grated
2 tablespoons cornstarch
1 (14 ounce) can chicken broth
1½ cups cooked broccoli florets
¾ cup diced, cooked carrots
1 teaspoon Worcestershire sauce
¼ teaspoon salt
¼ teaspoon white pepper
½ teaspoon garlic powder
2 cups half-and-half cream

In large saucepan, saute onion and bell pepper in butter.
Mix cheese and cornstarch.

To onion and peppers, add broth, cheese-cornstarch
mixture, a little at a time, and heat until cheese melts.
Stir until smooth and add ham, broccoli, carrots,
Worcestershire sauce, salt, white pepper and garlic powder.

Cook over low heat while adding half-and-half cream.
Serve with sprig of watercress. Serves 6 to 8.

Bingo Black Bean Soup

2 cups dried black beans, washed, soaked overnight,
   drained
1 cup diced ham
1 onion, chopped
1 carrot, chopped
2 ribs celery, chopped
3 jalapeno peppers, seeded, chopped
2 (14 ounce) cans chicken broth
10 cups water
2 teaspoons cumin
1 teaspoon salt
2 tablespoons snipped fresh cilantro
1 teaspoon oregano
1 teaspoon chili powder
1 teaspoon cayenne pepper
1 (8 ounce) carton sour cream

In large, heavy soup pot, place all ingredients except sour
cream. Bring to a boil, turn heat down and simmer for
3 hours or until beans are tender.

Add more water as needed and stir occasionally.
Make sure there is enough water in pot to make soup
consistency and not too thick.

Place few cups at a time in food processor (using steel
blade) or blender and puree until smooth. Add sour cream
and reheat soup. Serve in individual bowls.

Corn-Ham Chowder

This is a great recipe to use when you have leftover ham!

3 medium potatoes
2 (14 ounce) cans chicken broth, divided
5 tablespoons butter
2 ribs celery, chopped
1 onion, chopped
4 tablespoons flour
1 (4 ounce) can chopped green chilies, drained
½ teaspoon white pepper
½ teaspoon salt
1 teaspoon seasoned salt
¼ teaspoon garlic powder
1 (16 ounce) package frozen corn
1 (16 ounce) can cream-style corn
1 (16 ounce) carton half-and-half cream
3 cups bite-sized cubed ham
2 cups shredded cheddar cheese

Peel potatoes, cut in small chunks and cook with 1 can chicken broth.

In large kettle, melt butter and saute celery and onion. Add flour and stir. Add remaining can of chicken broth, stir constantly and heat until slightly thick.

Add drained, cooked potatoes and remaining ingredients. Heat slowly and stir several times to keep from sticking.

This will only serve 6 to 8 because everyone will want a second bowl.

White Lightning Chili

1½ cups dried navy beans
3 (14 ounce) cans chicken broth
2 tablespoons (¼ stick) butter
1 cup water
1 onion, chopped
1 clove garlic, minced
3 cups chopped, cooked chicken
1 (4 ounce) can chopped green chilies, drained
½ teaspoon sweet basil
½ teaspoon white pepper
1½ teaspoons ground cumin
½ teaspoon dried oregano
⅛ teaspoon cayenne pepper
⅛ teaspoon ground cloves
6 (8-inch) flour tortillas
Grated Monterey Jack cheese
Salsa, optional

Sort, wash beans and place in Dutch oven. Cover with water 2 inches above beans, soak overnight and drain. Add broth, butter, water, onion and garlic. Bring to a boil, reduce heat and cover. Simmer for 2 hours, 30 minutes and stir occasionally.

With potato masher, mash beans until at least half beans are mashed. Add chicken, green chilies, basil, white pepper, cumin, oregano, cayenne pepper and cloves. Bring to a boil, reduce heat and cover. Simmer another 30 minutes.

With kitchen shears, make 4 cuts in each tortilla toward center, but not completely through center. Line serving bowls with tortillas and overlap cut edges. Spoon in chili and top with cheese or salsa.

Pancho Villa Stew

3 cups diced, cooked ham
1 pound smoked sausage, cut in ½-inch slices
3 (14 ounce) cans chicken broth
1 (15 ounce) can whole tomatoes, with liquid
3 (4 ounce) cans chopped green chilies, with liquid
1 large onion, chopped
1 teaspoon garlic powder
2 teaspoons ground cumin
2 teaspoons cocoa
1 teaspoon dried oregano
½ teaspoon salt
2 (15 ounce) cans pinto beans, with liquid
1 (15 ounce) can hominy, with liquid
1 (8 ounce) can whole kernel corn, with liquid
Flour tortillas

In roaster, combine ham, sausage, broth, tomatoes, green chilies, onion, garlic powder, cumin, cocoa, oregano and salt. Bring to a boil and then reduce heat. Simmer for 45 minutes.

Add pinto beans, hominy and corn and bring to a boil. Reduce heat and simmer another 15 minutes. Serve with buttered flour tortillas or cornbread.

Santa Fe Stew

1½ pounds ground round beef
1 (1 ounce) package taco seasoning
1 (1 ounce) package original ranch-style dressing mix
1 (15 ounce) can whole kernel corn, with liquid
1 (15 ounce) can kidney beans, with liquid
2 (15 ounce) cans stewed tomatoes, with liquid
2 (15 ounce) cans pinto beans, with liquid
1 (4 ounce) can diced green chilies and tomatoes

Brown beef and drain, if necessary. Add both packages of
seasonings and mix well. Add corn, kidney beans, stewed
tomatoes, pinto beans, green chilies and tomatoes and mix
well.

Simmer for about 25 minutes. If you want it really hot, use
2 cans green chilies and tomatoes.

Special Spinach Sandwiches

2 (10 ounce) packages frozen chopped spinach, thawed
1 (8 ounce) package cream cheese, softened
1 cup mayonnaise
2 hard-boiled eggs, mashed
1 (1 ounce) package dry vegetable soup mix
¾ cup chopped pecans

Drain spinach VERY well, mash it to squeeze out more
water and press it between several pieces of paper towels.

(Continued on next page.)

(Continued)

Place cream cheese in mixing bowl and beat until smooth. Add mayonnaise and beat until mixture mixes well. Stir in mashed eggs, soup mix and pecans.

Chill for several hours before spreading sandwiches. This will make large loaf of bread into sandwiches.

Easy-Going Hot Bunwiches
Now you can have Sunday night supper ready in the freezer.

8 hamburger buns
8 slices Swiss cheese
8 slices ham
8 slices turkey
8 slices American cheese

Lay out all 8 buns. On bottom, place slices of Swiss cheese, then ham, turkey and American cheese. Place top bun over American cheese slice.

Wrap each sandwich individually in foil and place in freezer. When ready to serve, remove from freezer 2 to 3 hours before serving.

Heat at 325° for 30 to 40 minutes and serve hot.

Tip: Instead of ham and turkey, use thin-sliced deli meats such as pastrami or corned beef. Switch cheese to slices of Mexican cheese.

Mouth-Water' Reuben Sandwiches

½ cup mayonnaise
1 tablespoon chili sauce
12 slices rye bread
12 slices corned beef
6 slices Swiss cheese
1 (16 ounce) can sauerkraut, well-drained
Butter, softened

Mix mayonnaise and chili sauce and spread over 6 slices of rye bread. Add slice of corned beef and cheese and then second slice of corned beef and sauerkraut.

Top with remaining bread slices and spread top slices with layer of butter. Place sandwiches, butter-side down in skillet and spread top of bread with butter.

Cook sandwiches uncovered over low heat for 10 minutes or until bottom is brown. Turn and cook until golden brown and cheese melts.

Pimento Cheese Party Sticks

12 slices whole wheat bread
2½ cups grated sharp cheddar cheese
⅓ cup chili sauce
¾ cup mayonnaise
½ cup chopped olives
½ cup chopped pecans
1 (2 ounce) jar chopped pimentos, drained
¼ teaspoon garlic powder

Trim crusts off bread. Combine all remaining ingredients and mix well.

Spread mixture on 6 slices of bread and top with remaining bread slices. Cut each sandwich into 3 strips and chill.

Festive Mango Salad

1 (3 ounce) package apricot gelatin
2 (3 ounce) packages lemon gelatin
1¾ cups boiling water
1 (8 ounce) package cream cheese, softened
2 (15 ounce) cans mangoes, reserve juice

Dissolve gelatin mixes in boiling water. In mixing bowl, beat cream cheese until creamy. Add mangoes and juice and beat (canned mangoes are soft and will beat well) until mangoes are just like pieces.

Add mango mixture into gelatin and pour into sprayed (2-quart) mold. It will make 12 to 14 little individual molds if you prefer.

Tip: This could make a delightful light dessert molded in a sherbet dish with a little shortbread cookie placed on the dessert plate.

Berry Pizzazz

1 (6 ounce) package blackberry gelatin
1 cup boiling water
1 (8 ounce) can crushed pineapple, with juice
1 (20 ounce) can blueberry pie filling

Topping:
1 (8 ounce) package cream cheese, softened
1 (6 ounce) carton blueberry yogurt
Chopped pecans

In mixing bowl, dissolve gelatin in boiling water and stir well. Fold in pineapple and pie filling and pour into 9 x 13-inch dish. Chill until firm.

For topping, beat cream cheese and yogurt and spread on top of gelatin mixture. Top with pecans.

Perfect Pistachio Salad

Perfect to serve on St. Patrick's Day.

1 (15 ounce) can crushed pineapple, drained
1 (11 ounce) can mandarin oranges, drained
1 (6 ounce) package pistachio instant pudding
2 cups miniature marshmallows
1 cup chopped pecans
1 cup flaked coconut, optional
1 (12 ounce) carton whipped topping

Combine pineapple, oranges, pudding, marshmallows, pecans and coconut and blend well.

Fold in whipped topping and chill. Serve in crystal bowl. Serves 8 to 10.

Fantastic Fruit Salad

This is a wonderful fruit salad for special holiday dinners.

2 (11 ounce) cans mandarin oranges
2 (15 ounce) cans pineapple chunks
1 (16 ounce) package frozen strawberries, thawed, drained
1 (20 ounce) can peach pie filling
1 (20 ounce) can apricot pie filling
2 bananas, sliced

Drain oranges, pineapple and strawberries. In mixing bowl, combine oranges, pineapple, strawberries, peach pie filling, apricot pie filling and bananas and gently mix.

Place mixture in crystal bowl for serving. Serves 16.

Chilled Ambrosia Salad
This is really a make-ahead ambrosia salad.

2 (1 ounce) packages unflavored gelatin
½ cup cold water
1 (20 ounce) can crushed pineapple
⅔ cup sugar
3 tablespoons lemon juice
1 (8 ounce) package cream cheese, softened
2 (11 ounce) cans mandarin oranges, drained
⅔ cup chopped pecans
½ cup flaked coconut

Mix gelatin with cold water. Drain pineapple and add enough water to juice to make 1 cup. Place juice in saucepan and heat to a boil. Add gelatin mixture and stir until gelatin dissolves.

Remove from heat, stir in sugar, lemon juice and cream cheese and blend with whisk.

Chill until mixture is consistency of egg whites (1 hour in refrigerator, but stir several times to check). Fold in pineapple, oranges, pecans and coconut. Serves 8.

Merry Mix Salad

3 (15 ounce) cans fruit cocktail, with juice
1 (14 ounce) can pineapple chunks, with juice
2 (3 ounce) packages dry, coconut-cream instant
   pudding mix
1 cup pecan halves, slightly broken by hand
1 (20 ounce) can cherry pie filling
1 (8 ounce) carton whipped topping
A few drops of red food coloring

In large bowl, combine fruit cocktail, pineapple chunks and pudding mix. Add pecans and cherry pie filling and fold in whipped topping with drops of red food coloring.

Place mixture in crystal dish and cover.

Tip: Serve this recipe as a dessert for company. Just spoon into parfait glasses, cover with plastic wrap and have it ready in refrigerator.

Sunny Pineapple-Raspberry Salad

1 (6 ounce) package lime gelatin
1 (8 ounce) can crushed pineapple, reserve juice from
  pineapple plus water to make 1 cup
1 (8 ounce) package cream cheese, softened
1 cup miniature marshmallows
1 (8 ounce) carton whipped topping
1 (6 ounce) package raspberry gelatin
1 cup boiling water
1 (12 ounce) package frozen raspberries, thawed
1 (8 ounce) can crushed pineapple, with juice

In large mixing bowl, dissolve lime gelatin with 1 cup
boiling pineapple juice and water. Add cream cheese and
beat on slow speed with mixer. Fold in marshmallows
and pineapple, chill for 30 minutes and fold in whipped
topping.

Pour into sprayed 9 x 13-inch glass dish and chill until set.

In separate bowl, dissolve raspberry gelatin with boiling
water. Add raspberries and crushed pineapple, pour over
first layer of gelatin mixture and chill until firm.

*Tip: If you like strawberries better than raspberries, use
strawberries and of course change raspberry gelatin to
strawberry gelatin.*

Cherry-Cranberry Salad

Nothing could be easier! This can be served anytime of year not just at Thanksgiving and Christmas.

1 (6 ounce) package cherry gelatin
1 cup boiling water
1 (20 ounce) can cherry pie filling
1 (16 ounce) can whole cranberry sauce

In mixing bowl, dissolve gelatin in boiling water and stir well. Mix pie filling and cranberry sauce into gelatin.

Pour in 9 x 13-inch dish and chill. Serve on lettuce leaves. Serves 8 to 10.

Happy Holiday Salad

2 (3 ounce) packages cream cheese, softened
2 tablespoons mayonnaise
2 tablespoons sugar
1 (16 ounce) can whole cranberry sauce
1 (8 ounce) can crushed pineapple, drained
½ cup chopped pecans
1 cup tiny marshmallows
1 (8 ounce) carton whipped topping

In mixing bowl combine cream cheese, mayonnaise and sugar and beat until creamy. Add fruit, pecans and marshmallows. Fold in whipped topping, pour into sprayed 9 x 13-inch shallow glass dish and freeze.

When ready to serve, take salad out of freezer few minutes before you cut into squares.

Fairy Blueberry Chill

First Layer:

1 (6 ounce) package lemon gelatin
1 cup boiling water
1 (8 ounce) package cream cheese, softened
3 tablespoons powdered sugar
1 (8 ounce) can crushed pineapple, with juice
1 cup half-and-half cream

Second Layer:

1 (6 ounce) package black-raspberry gelatin
1 cup boiling water
1 (15 ounce) can blueberries, drained
1 (20 ounce) can blueberry pie filling

In mixing bowl, dissolve lemon gelatin in boiling water and mix well. Add cream cheese and powdered sugar and heat, slowly at first, until mixture is smooth. Add pineapple and half-and-half cream and pour into sprayed 9 x 13-inch dish. Chill until gelatin is firm.

Dissolve black-raspberry gelatin (you could also use black-cherry gelatin) in boiling water. Stir in drained blueberries and blueberry pie filling and mix well. Pour over lemon gelatin mixture and chill several hours before serving.

Serve on lettuce leaf and place blueberry mixture on bottom. Serves 12.

Incredible Strawberry Salad
It really is incredible!

2 (8 ounce) packages cream cheese, softened
2 tablespoons mayonnaise
½ cup powdered sugar
1 (16 ounce) package frozen strawberries, thawed
1 (10 ounce) package small marshmallows
1 (8 ounce) can crushed pineapple, drained
1 (8 ounce) carton whipped topping
1 cup chopped pecans

In large mixing bowl, combine cream cheese, mayonnaise and powdered sugar and beat until creamy. Fold in strawberries (if strawberries are large, cut in half), marshmallows, pineapple, whipped topping and pecans.

Pour into 9 x 13-inch glass dish and freeze. Take out of freezer 15 minutes before you cut and serve. Serves 12.

Divine Divinity Salad

1 (6 ounce) package lemon gelatin
¾ cup boiling water
1 (8 ounce) package cream cheese, softened
2 tablespoons sugar
¾ cup chopped pecans
1 (15 ounce) can crushed pineapple, with juice
1 (8 ounce) carton whipped topping

In mixing bowl, combine gelatin with boiling water and dissolve well. Cool slightly, add cream cheese and beat at very slow speed.

Add sugar, pecans and pineapple and cool. Fold in whipped topping, pour into 9 x 13-inch dish and chill. Serves 12.

Famous Artichoke Salad

1 (1 ounce) package unflavored gelatin
¼ cup cold water
½ cup boiling water
1 cup mayonnaise
1 (14 ounce) can hearts of artichoke, well-drained
½ (10 ounce) package frozen green peas, thawed,
  uncooked
2 tablespoons lemon juice
1 (4 ounce) jar chopped pimentos, drained
1 bunch green onions with tops, finely chopped
1½ cups shredded mozzarella cheese
1 teaspoon Italian herb seasoning
⅛ teaspoon cayenne pepper
½ teaspoon garlic powder
Paprika

Soften gelatin in cold water, add boiling water and mix
well. Add mayonnaise and stir until smooth.

Remove any spikes or tough leaves from artichoke hearts
and chop. Add all remaining ingredients except paprika.
Pour into ring mold and chill.

When ready to serve, slip knife around edges to loosen
from mold. Unmold onto serving plate lined with lettuce.
Sprinkle paprika over salad.

*Tip: You could put radishes, olives or black olives in center
of mold when serving.*

Emerald Isle Salad

I like this salad best when you can get fresh cucumbers from the garden or Farmer's Market and the best cucumbers are those long and "skinny" ones with very few seeds.

1 (3 ounce) package lime gelatin
¾ cup boiling water
1 cup peeled, shredded, seeded cucumber
2 teaspoons finely grated onion
1 tablespoons finely grated onion
1 tablespoon lemon juice
¼ teaspoon salt
1 cup mayonnaise
1 cup cream style small-curd cottage cheese
1 (2½ ounce) package slivered almonds, toasted

Dissolve gelatin in water and cool. Add cucumber, onion, lemon juice, salt, mayonnaise, cottage cheese and almonds.

Pour into individual molds or into 9-inch dish. Chill 8 hours. Serves 8.

Creamy Gazpacho Salad

This is delicious! Wonderful when you want a make-ahead salad – but not a sweet salad.

1 (10 ounce) can tomato soup
1 (1 ounce) package unflavored gelatin
¼ cup cold water
1 (8 ounce) package cream cheese, softened
½ cup chopped celery
½ cup chopped bell pepper
1 tablespoon finely chopped onion
1 teaspoon lemon juice
½ cup chopped pecans
1 cup mayonnaise
⅓ cup sliced green olives

On medium heat, blend soup, gelatin and water. Add cream cheese, stir constantly while on medium heat and blend well. Cool and add remaining ingredients.

Pour mixture into mold or 9 x 9-inch glass dish and chill overnight. Cut into squares to serve. Serves 8.

Tip: To make a main dish out of this recipe, add 1 cup cooked shrimp.

Fancy Potato Salad

2 (1 ounce) packages unflavored gelatin
1 cup buttermilk
8 cups cubed, cooked potatoes
6 hard boiled eggs, diced
2 cups chopped celery
¾ cup chopped green onion with tops
1 (2 ounce) jar pimientos, drained
1 (8 ounce) carton sour cream
2 tablespoons sugar
1 tablespoon prepared mustard
1 tablespoon salt
¼ heaping teaspoon pepper
1 teaspoon seasoned salt

Oil 1 (12-cup) bundt pan. In saucepan, combine gelatin and buttermilk and heat over medium heat. Stir until gelatin dissolves and cool.

In large bowl, combine remaining ingredients with gelatin mixture and place firmly into place in pan. Cover and chill until set.

To unmold, use thin, narrow knife and loosen center core of salad. Dip pan in hot water for 10 seconds and turn out on serving plate. Garnish with celery leaves around edges of serving dish.

Broccoli Salad Supreme

The grapes give the recipe a special "zip".

1 large bunch broccoli cut in bite-size pieces
1 cup chopped celery
1 bunch green onions with tops, sliced
½ red bell pepper, chopped
1 cup halved, seedless green grapes
1 cup halved, seedless red grapes
1 cup slivered almonds, toasted
½ pound bacon, cooked crisp, drained, crumbled

Dressing:

1 cup mayonnaise
¼ cup sugar
2 tablespoons vinegar
1 teaspoon salt
½ teaspoon black pepper

Wash and drain broccoli well. It will help to drain broccoli if you place pieces on cup towel, pick it up and shake well.

Combine all ingredients and toss. Combine and mix dressing ingredients, add to salad and toss. Chill. Serves 8 to 10.

Cauliflower-Broccoli Crunch

This is one of my most favorite salads. It goes well with just about everything.

1 (8 ounce) carton sour cream
1 cup mayonnaise
1 (1 ounce) package ranch style dressing mix
1 large head cauliflower, broken into bite-size pieces
1 large bunch fresh broccoli, broken into bite-size pieces
1 (10 ounce) box frozen green peas, thawed, uncooked
3 ribs celery, sliced
1 bunch green onions with tops, chopped
1 (8 ounce) can water chestnuts, drained
⅓ cup sweet relish, drained
8 ounces mozzarella cheese, cut in chunks
2 (2½ ounce) packages slivered almonds, toasted

Mix sour cream, mayonnaise and dressing mix and set aside. MAKE SURE cauliflower and broccoli are WELL DRAINED.

In large container combine salad ingredients, add dressing and toss. Chill. Serves 12.

Quick Broccoli-Noodle Salad

Who thought up the idea of grating broccoli "stems" for a salad? It was
pure genius! This salad is different – and very good. It will last and
still be "crispy" in the refrigerator for days!

1 cup slivered almonds, toasted
1 cup sunflower seeds, toasted
2 (.3 ounce) packages chicken-flavored Ramen noodles
1 (12 ounce) package broccoli slaw

Dressing:

¾ cup oil
½ cup white vinegar
½ cup sugar
Ramen noodles seasoning packet

Preheat oven to 275°. Toast almonds and sunflower seeds
in oven for 15 minutes. Break up ramen noodles (but do
not cook) and mix with slaw, almonds and sunflower seeds.

In separate bowl, combine dressing ingredients and noodle
seasoning packet. Pour over slaw mixture and mix well.
Prepare at least 1 hour before serving.

Crunchy Chinese Slaw

1 head green cabbage, grated
½ head red cabbage, grated
1 cup slivered almonds, toasted
1 bunch green onions, sliced
1 large green bell pepper, diced
1 cup sliced celery
1 (11 ounce) can mandarin oranges, drained
2 (.3 ounce) packages chicken-flavored Ramon noodles, crumbled
1 cup sunflower seeds

Dressing:

1 cup oil
¾ tarragon vinegar
¾ cup sugar
2 teaspoons salt
1 teaspoon pepper
¾ teaspoon seasoned salt
2 dashes hot sauce (optional)

Preheat oven to 275°. Toast almonds in oven for 15 minutes.

Combine cabbage, almonds, onion, bell peppers, celery, oranges, noodles and sunflower seeds in bowl. In separate large bowl, mix all dressing ingredients and pour over cabbage mixture. Toss well. Serves about 18.

Tip: I splurge on cabbage and buy 2 heads of green cabbage and use only the outer, greenest leaves to equal one head green cabbage. For the red cabbage, I also cut only the outer red leaves.

Fresh Spinach Salad Special

½ cup oil
½ cup red wine vinegar
3 tablespoons ketchup
¼ cup sugar
1 teaspoon salt
½ teaspoon garlic powder
½ teaspoon dry mustard
Pepper
1 (10 ounce) package fresh spinach
4 hard-boiled eggs, sliced
8 slices bacon, crisply cooked, crumbled
1 cup fresh mushrooms, sliced
1 red onion, thinly sliced
1 (8 ounce) can sliced water chestnuts, optional
Croutons

Combine first 8 ingredients to make dressing. Chill for at least 6 hours before serving. Wash, drain and tear spinach into bite-size pieces.

When ready to serve, toss spinach with eggs, bacon, mushrooms, onion and water chestnuts and add dressing. Top with croutons. Serves 8.

Orange-Almond Romaine

⅓ cup slivered almonds, toasted
2 (11 ounce) cans mandarin oranges, drained
1 bunch green onions with tops, chopped
2 heads romaine lettuce, torn in small pieces
1 cup packaged croutons

Dressing:

¼ cup sugar
1 teaspoon dry mustard
1 teaspoon salt
¼ cup cider vinegar
½ cup salad oil
2 tablespoons poppy seeds

Preheat oven to 275°. Toast almonds in oven for
15 minutes. Combine almonds, oranges, onion and lettuce
and mix well. Add croutons to salad when ready to serve.

To prepare dressing, mix all dressing ingredients. Add to
salad when ready to serve. Stir dressing well just before
adding to salad. Serves 6.

Crazy Bean Salad

1 (16 ounce) can green beans, drained
1 (16 ounce) can peas, drained
1 (16 ounce) can whole kernel white corn, drained
1 cup finely chopped celery
1 green pepper, chopped
1 bunch green onions, chopped
1 (2 ounce) jar chopped pimentos, drained

Dressing:

½ cup sugar
½ cup wine vinegar
½ cup oil
1 teaspoon salt
½ teaspoon pepper
½ teaspoon tarragon
½ teaspoon basil

Drain all vegetables and combine in bowl with lid.

To prepare dressing, mix all dressing ingredients and pour over vegetables. Cover and chill overnight. Salad can be stored in refrigerator for several days. Serves 8 to 10.

Winter Bean Medley

1 (16 ounce) can French-style green beans, drained
1 (16 ounce) can jalapeno black-eyed peas, drained
1 (16 ounce) can shoe peg white corn, drained
1 (16 ounce) can English peas, drained
1 (2 ounce) jar chopped pimentos, drained
1 bell pepper, chopped
1 onion, sliced, broken into rings

Dressing:

¾ cup sugar
1 teaspoon salt
1 teaspoon seasoned salt
½ teaspoon garlic powder
1 teaspoon seasoned pepper
½ cup oil
¾ cup vinegar

In 3-quart container with lid, combine all salad ingredients and gently mix. Be sure to drain vegetables well before combining.

To prepare dressing, mix all dressing ingredients, pour over vegetables and stir. Cover and chill. Serves 16.

Tip: I keep a supply of these ingredients on hand – and when you need to take a dish to a friend – it's a salad in a hurry.

Lucky Black-Eyed Pea Salad

2 (16 ounce) cans jalapeno black-eyed peas, drained
1 ripe avocado, peeled, chopped
½ purple onion, chopped
1 cup chopped celery
1 bell pepper, chopped

Dressing:

⅓ cup oil
⅓ cup white vinegar
3 tablespoons sugar
¼ teaspoon garlic powder
½ teaspoon salt

In large bowl, combine all salad ingredients and mix well.

To prepare dressing, mix dressing ingredients and add to vegetables. Toss and chill. Serves 10.

Cornbread Salad Surprise

2 (6 ounce) packages Mexican cornbread mix
2 eggs
1⅓ cup milk
2 ribs celery, sliced
1 bunch green onions with tops, chopped
1 green bell pepper, chopped
2 firm tomatoes, chopped, drained
8 slices bacon, cooked, crumbled
1 cup grated cheddar cheese
1 (8 ounce) can whole kernel corn, drained
½ cup ripe olives, chopped, optional
2½ cups mayonnaise

Prepare cornbread with eggs and milk according to package directions. Cook, cool and crumble cornbread in large mixing bowl.

Add celery, green onions, bell pepper, tomatoes, bacon, cheese, corn, olives and mayonnaise and mix well. Serves 16.

Nutty Fruit Salad

2 medium apples, cored, chopped
¾ cup halved, seedless green grapes
½ cup chopped celery
½ cup chopped pecans
½ cup sunflower seeds
⅓ cup mayonnaise
1 banana, sliced
Lettuce leaves

In medium mixing bowl, toss apples, grapes, celery, pecans and sunflower seeds. Fold in mayonnaise and banana.

Serve on individual lettuce-lined salad plates. It may also be served in a crystal bowl. Serves 6.

Chicken-Salad Squares

5 chicken breasts, cooked, finely chopped
2 tablespoons unflavored gelatin
½ cup water
1 (15 ounce) can chicken broth
1 (8 ounce) package cream cheese, softened
1 cup mayonnaise
1 (4 ounce) jar pimentos, drained
1 cup slivered almonds, toasted
3 tablespoons capers
3 hard-boiled eggs, chopped
1½ cups chopped celery
½ teaspoon salt
½ teaspoon white pepper

Mix gelatin with water and set aside. Bring broth to boil, dissolve in hot broth and remove from heat.

With mixer, beat cream cheese and mayonnaise until creamy. Fold in chicken, pimentos, almonds, capers, eggs, celery, salt, white pepper and gelatin.

Pour into sprayed 9 x 13-inch dish. Chill several hours before cutting in squares. Serve on lettuce leaf. Serves 8 to 10.

Tip: You can also use canned chicken, drained, instead of chicken breasts but you will need 2 (12 ounce) cans.

Cranberry-Chicken Salad

Layer 1:
1½ (1 ounce) packages unflavored gelatin
¼ cup cold water
1 (16 ounce) can whole cranberry sauce
1 (8 ounce) can crushed pineapple
¼ cup sugar
1 cup chopped pecans
Red food coloring, optional

Layer 2:
1½ (1 ounce) packages unflavored gelatin
¼ cup cold water
½ cup water
1 (3 ounce) package cream cheese
3 tablespoons lemon juice
¾ teaspoon salt
2 cups diced, cooked chicken
¾ cup chopped celery
¼ cup sweet relish
1 cup chopped pecans

LAYER 1:
Soften gelatin in cold water. Place cranberry sauce, pineapple and sugar in saucepan and heat to a boil. Add gelatin mixture and stir well.

Mix in pecans and red food coloring. Pour into sprayed 9 x 13-inch glass dish and chill.

LAYER 2:
Soften gelatin in ¼ cup cold water. Add ½ cup water, cream cheese, lemon juice and salt to saucepan and heat to a boil. Stir until cream cheese dissolves. Add to gelatin mixture.

(Continued on next page.)

(Continued)

Fold in chicken, celery, relish and pecans. Pour over cranberry mixture and chill. To serve, cut into squares and put cranberry side up on bed of lettuce.

Southwestern Chicken Salad

4 cups cubed, cooked chicken breasts
1 (16 ounce) can black beans, drained
¾ red onion, chopped
½ red bell pepper, chopped
½ yellow bell pepper, chopped
¼ cup chopped fresh cilantro
½ cup sour cream
¼ cup mayonnaise
½ teaspoon garlic powder
1 jalapeno pepper, finely chopped
1 teaspoon lime juice
1 teaspoon salt
½ teaspoon pepper
½ cup pine nuts, toasted

Combine chicken, beans, onion, bell peppers and cilantro in large bowl.

In small bowl, whisk sour cream and mayonnaise. Stir in garlic powder, jalapeno pepper and lime juice and add to large bowl of chicken. Add salt and pepper and toss.

Chill at least 1 hour.

Just before serving, toss in pine nuts. Serve on bed of lettuce. Serves 8.

Simply Scrumptious Shrimp Salad

3 cups chopped, cooked shrimp
1 cup chopped celery
4 hard-boiled eggs, chopped
½ cup sliced green stuffed olives, well drained
¼ cup sliced green onions
¼ cup chopped dill pickle
1 cup mayonnaise
2 tablespoons chili sauce
1 tablespoon horseradish
1 teaspoon seasoned salt
¾ teaspoon seasoned pepper

Combine all ingredients, toss lightly and chill.
Serves 6 to 8.

Chilled Shrimp Mousse
This could also be served at a luncheon.

1 (10 ounce) can tomato soup
2 (1 ounce) packages unflavored gelatin
⅓ cup cold water
1 (8 ounce) package cream cheese, softened
½ cup chopped celery
½ cup chopped bell pepper
2 tablespoons finely chopped onion
1 teaspoon lemon juice
½ cup chopped pecans
1 cup mayonnaise
⅓ cup sliced green olives, optional
1 tablespoon white wine Worcestershire sauce
2 (4 ounce) cans deveined shrimp, drained

Heat soup, gelatin and water and blend well. Add cream
cheese and stir constantly while leaving on low heat until
cream cheese melts. Blend well.

(Continued on next page.)

(Continued)

Cool and add remaining ingredients. Pour mixture into shell or fish mold. Chill overnight. Serve with crackers. Serves 8.

Cool and add remaining ingredients. Pour mixture into shell or fish mold. Chill overnight. Serve with crackers. Serves 8.

Hawaiian Chicken Salad

1 cup cooked rice
3½ cups cubed, cooked chicken breasts
2 cups diced celery
1 (8 ounce) can water chestnuts, drained, chopped
1 (15 ounce) cans pineapple tidbits, well drained
1 (3 ounce) can flaked coconut
1 banana, sliced

Dressing:

1¾ to 2 cups mayonnaise
2 tablespoons lemon juice
¼ teaspoon salt
½ teaspoon white pepper
1 teaspoon curry powder

Combine all ingredients in large mixing bowl and mix well.

To prepare dressing, combine all dressing ingredients and fold into chicken salad mixture. Chill several hours before serving. Serves 10.

Delicious Tuna Salad

This is an "old-time" recipe but still a favorite.
It is a wonderful luncheon treat!

3 (1 ounce) packages unflavored gelatin
½ cup cold water
1 (10 ounce) can cream of chicken soup
2 (6 ounce) cans tuna, rinsed
1 cup mayonnaise
1 cup chopped celery
3 hard-boiled eggs, chopped
1½ teaspoons Worcestershire sauce
½ cup chopped stuffed olives

Mix gelatin and water and dissolve well. In medium saucepan, heat soup and stir in gelatin. Mix well and set aside.

In mixing bowl, combine tuna, mayonnaise, celery, eggs, Worcestershire sauce and olives and mix well. Add soup mixture and pour into sprayed 7 x 11-inch baking dish.

Refrigerate several hours before serving.

Vegetables & Side Dishes

Broccoli-Cauliflower Bake

1 (10 ounce) package frozen broccoli spears
1 (10 ounce) package frozen cauliflower
1 egg
⅔ cup mayonnaise
1 (10 ounce) can cream of chicken soup, undiluted
1 cup grated Swiss cheese
1 onion, chopped
1 cup dry, seasoned breadcrumbs
2 tablespoons (¼ stick) butter
Paprika

Preheat oven to 350°. Cook broccoli and cauliflower according to package directions. Drain well and place in large mixing bowl.

In saucepan, combine egg, mayonnaise and soup and heat well. Pour mixture over vegetables, add cheese and onion and mix well.

Pour into buttered 9 x 13-inch baking dish. Combine breadcrumbs and butter and add to mixture. Sprinkle paprika over top. Bake for 30 to 35 minutes. Serves 8 to 10.

Cauliflower Medley

1 large head cauliflower
1 (16 ounce) can Italian recipe stewed tomatoes
1 onion, finely chopped
1 green bell pepper, diced
1 tablespoon sugar
1 teaspoon salt
½ teaspoon black pepper
1 tablespoon cornstarch
¼ cup (½ stick) butter, melted
1 cup grated cheddar cheese
¾ cup crackers or dry breadcrumbs

Preheat oven to 350°. Break cauliflower into pieces and cook in large saucepan with salt water for 10 minutes or until tender crisp and drain well.

Add stewed tomatoes, onion, bell pepper, sugar, salt, black pepper, cornstarch and melted butter.

Transfer mixture to 2-quart casserole baking dish and sprinkle cheese and crumbs over top. Bake for 35 minutes. Serves 8.

Muy Bien Cauliflower Con Queso

1 large head cauliflower, broken into florets
¼ cup (½ stick) butter
½ onion, chopped
2 tablespoons flour
1 (16 ounce) can Mexican recipe stewed tomatoes
1 (4 ounce) can chopped green chilies, drained
¾ teaspoon seasoned pepper
1 teaspoon salt
1½ cups grated Monterey Jack cheese

Cook florets until crisp-tender, drain and set aside. Melt butter in medium saucepan and add onion and cook until clear.

Blend in flour then stir in tomatoes. Cook until mixture is thick and stir constantly. Add green chilies, seasoned pepper and salt. Fold in cheese and stir until it melts.

Pour sauce over drained hot cauliflower and serve. Serves 6 to 8.

Tip: *If you prefer to cook the cauliflower earlier, place it in a serving dish and microwave cauliflower about 15 seconds, just enough to warm. Pour tomato-cheese mixture over cauliflower. Use plain stewed tomatoes if you do not want a hot taste.*

Fiesta Corn

1 (16 ounce) can cream-style corn
1 (16 ounce) can whole kernel corn, drained
1 bell pepper, chopped
1 small onion, chopped
1 (4 ounce) can chopped green chilies, drained
2 tablespoons (¼ stick) butter, melted
2 eggs
1 tablespoon sugar
½ teaspoon salt
½ teaspoon pepper
½ cup buttery cracker crumbs
2 tablespoons grated parmesan cheese
1 cup grated cheddar cheese

Topping:

¾ cup buttery cracker crumbs
2 tablespoons grated parmesan cheese
Paprika to garnish

Grease 9 x 13-inch baking dish. In large mixing bowl, combine all ingredients except topping and pour into baking dish.

Top with cracker crumbs and parmesan and garnish with paprika. Bake for 45 minutes in 350° oven. Serves 8 to 10.

Green Bean Bonanza

3 (16 ounce) cans French-cut green beans
1 cup sour cream
½ (16 ounce) carton jalapeno processed cheese, cut in
   chunks
½ onion, minced
½ teaspoon pepper
2 cups crushed crispy rice cereal
3 tablespoons butter, melted

Preheat oven to 350°. Drain green beans well. Butter
2½-quart baking dish.

In large saucepan, melt sour cream and jalapeno cheese.
Stir constantly. Add onion, pepper and green beans and
mix well.

Pour into prepared baking dish. Combine crushed crispy
rice cereal and butter, sprinkle over green bean mixture
and bake for 30 minutes. Serves 8 to 10.

Tip: Corn flake cereal works well also.

Best-Ever Baked Beans

2 (16 ounce) cans pork and beans, slightly drained
1 tablespoon Worcestershire sauce
½ onion, chopped
⅔ cup packed brown sugar
3 dashes hot sauce
1 teaspoon prepared mustard
1¼ cups ketchup
3 strips bacon

Preheat oven to 350°. In mixing bowl, combine beans,
Worcestershire sauce, onion, sugar, hot sauce, mustard
and ketchup and mix well.

(Continued on next page.)

(Continued)

Pour into sprayed casserole baking dish and place bacon strips over beans. Bake for 45 to 50 minutes. Serves 8.

Wild West Corn

1 (8 ounce) package cream cheese
½ cup sour cream
½ cup milk
1 (4 ounce) can chopped green chilies, drained
1 teaspoon salt
1 teaspoon white pepper
1 (2 ounce) jar pimentos, drained
3 (15 ounce) cans whole kernel corn, drained
¼ teaspoon hot sauce
1 cup cracker crumbs

Preheat oven to 350°. In large saucepan, melt cream cheese, sour cream and milk and stir constantly. Add green chilies, salt, pepper, pimentos, corn and hot sauce and mix well.

Pour into buttered 2½-quart baking dish and bake covered for 25 minutes. Sprinkle cracker crumbs over casserole and cook uncovered for 10 minutes longer. Serves 8 to 10.

Green Bean Supreme

2 tablespoons (¼ stick) butter
1 (10 ounce) can cream of mushroom soup
1 (3 ounce) package cream cheese, softened
3 (16 ounce) cans French-style green beans, drained
1 tablespoon dried onion flakes
1 (8 ounce) can sliced water chestnuts, drained
½ teaspoon garlic powder
½ teaspoon seasoned salt
1½ cups grated cheddar cheese
1 cup cracker crumbs
1 (2 ounce) package slivered almonds

Preheat oven to 350°. Melt butter in large saucepan and add soup and cream cheese. Cook over low heat and stir constantly until cream cheese melts and mixture is fairly smooth.

Remove from heat and stir in green beans, onion flakes, water chestnuts, garlic powder, seasoned salt and cheese and mix well.

Pour mixture into 9 x 13-inch casserole baking dish. Top with cracker crumbs and almonds. Bake uncovered for 30 minutes or until casserole bubbles around edges. Serves 8.

Pine Nut Green Beans

1 (16 ounce) package frozen green beans
¼ cup (½ stick) butter
¾ cup pine nuts
¼ teaspoon garlic powder
½ teaspoon salt
½ teaspoon black pepper
½ teaspoon celery salt

Cook beans in water in covered 3-quart saucepan for 10 to 15 minutes or until tender-crisp and drain.

Melt butter in skillet over medium heat and add pine nuts. Cook until golden brown and stir frequently. Add pine nuts to green beans and season with garlic powder, salt, black pepper and celery salt. Serves 8.

So-Good Almond-Asparagus Bake

5 (10 ounce) cans asparagus spears, divided
1½ cups cracker crumbs, divided
4 eggs, hard-boiled, sliced, divided
1½ cups grated cheddar cheese, divided
½ cup (1 stick) butter, melted
½ cup milk
2 (5 ounce) packages sliced almonds

Preheat oven to 350°. Drain asparagus and arrange half asparagus in sprayed 9 x 13-inch backing dish. Add layer of ¾ cup crumbs, half sliced eggs and sprinkle half cheese. Repeat process with remaining asparagus, crumbs and eggs.

Drizzle butter and milk over dish and top with almonds and remaining cheese. Bake for 30 minutes. Serves 10 to 12.

Confetti-Squash Casserole

1 pound yellow squash, sliced
1 pound zucchini, sliced
1 large onion, finely chopped
1 (10 ounce) can cream of chicken soup
1 (8 ounce) carton sour cream
1 (4 ounce) jar chopped pimentos, drained
1 (8 ounce) can sliced water chestnuts, drained
2 carrots, grated
½ cup (1 stick) butter
1 (6 ounce) package herb-seasoned stuffing mix

Cook squash, zucchini and onion in salt water for 10 minutes and drain well. Combine chicken soup, sour cream, pimentos, water chestnuts and carrots and mix gently.

Melt butter in saucepan, add stuffing and stir. Combine stuffing mix and squash mixture until it blends well. Cover and pour into sprayed 9 x 13-inch baking dish. Bake for 30 minutes. Serves 8 to 10.

Zippy Zucchini

4 eggs
2 cups grated Monterey Jack cheese
1 cup grated cheddar cheese
4 cups grated zucchini
1 (4 ounce) can chopped green chilies, drained
1 (2 ounce) jar sliced pimentos, optional
1 onion, finely chopped
1 teaspoon Creole seasoning
1 cup crushed croutons
⅓ cup grated parmesan cheese

Preheat oven to 350°. In large mixing bowl, beat eggs well. Stir in cheese, zucchini, green chilies, pimentos, onion and Creole seasoning and mix well.

(Continued on next page.)

(Continued)

Pour into sprayed 2-quart baking dish and bake uncovered for 35 minutes.

Mix crushed croutons and parmesan cheese. After 35 minutes, sprinkle crouton mixture over casserole and bake another 10 minutes. Serves 8.

Sweet Onion Casserole

3 cups cracker crumbs
½ cup (1 stick) butter, melted, divided
4 cups thinly sliced onions

Sauce:

1 cup milk
2 eggs, slightly beaten
1 teaspoon seasoned salt
¼ teaspoon pepper
1½ cups grated cheddar cheese

Preheat oven to 300°. Combine and mix cracker crumbs and ¼ cup butter. Place mixture in 9 x 13-inch baking dish and pat down. Sauté onions in remaining butter and spread over crust.

For sauce, combine milk, eggs, seasoned salt, pepper and cheese in saucepan. Over low heat, cook until cheese melts. Pour onions on crust and bake for 45 minutes or until knife inserted in center comes out clean.

Serve as replacement for potatoes or rice.

Yummy Yellow Squash

4 cups sliced, cooked, drained squash
1 (4 ounce) jar chopped pimentos, drained
1 carrot, grated
1 (8 ounce) can sliced water chestnuts, drained
1 cup sour cream
1 cup small-curd cottage cheese
1 (3 ounce) package cream cheese, softened
1½ cups Monterey Jack cheese
¼ cup (½ stick) butter, melted
1 (6 ounce) package chicken-flavor stuffing mix, divided

Preheat oven to 350°. After squash is drained well, add pimentos, carrot and water chestnuts and mix.

In another bowl mix sour cream, cottage cheese, cream cheese, Jack cheese and butter. Mix well with whisk.

Stir in half stuffing mix and all seasoning mix with stuffing. Fold into squash and spoon mixture into lightly sprayed 3-quart casserole baking dish.

Sprinkle remaining stuffing mix over top and bake for 30 to 35 minutes. Serves 8 to 10.

Cheesy Spinach Bake

2 (10 ounce) packages frozen, chopped spinach
1 (16 ounce) carton small-curd cottage cheese
2½ cups grated sharp cheddar cheese
4 eggs, beaten
3 tablespoons flour
¼ cup (½ stick) butter, melted
¼ teaspoon garlic salt
½ teaspoon lemon pepper
¼ teaspoon celery salt
1 tablespoon dried onion flakes

Preheat oven to 325°. Defrost spinach and squeeze out all water.

In large bowl, mix spinach, cottage cheese, cheddar cheese, eggs, flour, butter, seasonings and onion flakes.

Pour into sprayed 2½-quart baking dish and bake for 1 hour. Serves 8 to 10.

Tip: Prepare casserole a day ahead and bake when ready to serve.

Spectacular Spinach Enchiladas

These are so good and so much fun to make and serve!

2 (10 ounce) packages chopped spinach, thawed,
    pressed dry
1 (1 ounce) package dry onion soup mix
12 ounces shredded cheddar cheese, divided
12 ounces shredded Monterey Jack cheese or mozzarella,
    divided
12 flour tortillas
2 cups whipping cream

Preheat oven to 350°. (Make sure your spinach has all
water pressed out!) In medium bowl, combine spinach and
soup mix.

Blend in 6 ounces cheddar and Jack cheeses. Lay out
12 tortillas and place about 3 heaping tablespoons spinach
mixture down middle of tortilla and roll up. Place each
filled tortilla seam side down in sprayed 9 x 13-inch baking
dish.

Pour cream over enchiladas, sprinkle with remaining
cheeses and bake covered for 20 minutes. Uncover and
bake another 15 minutes longer. Serves 6 to 8.

*Tip: This recipe freezes well. To make ahead of time, freeze
    before adding cream and remaining cheeses. Thaw in
    refrigerator the night before cooking.*

Hot Vegetable Frittata

This makes an elegant dish; perfect for a brunch or late supper.

3 tablespoons oil
1 onion, chopped
¾ cup chopped red bell pepper
2 cups chopped zucchini
2 cups chopped yellow squash
¼ cup half-and-half cream
1 (8 ounce) package cream cheese, cubed
6 eggs
1 cup shredded mozzarella cheese
¾ teaspoon garlic powder
1 teaspoon salt
½ teaspoon black pepper
2 teaspoons white wine Worcestershire sauce
1 cup dry, seasoned breadcrumbs
2 tablespoons (¼ stick) butter, melted

Preheat oven to 350°. In large skillet, heat oil and sauté onion, bell peppers, zucchini and yellow squash. Cook just until tender-crisp, remove from heat and set aside to cool.

In mixing bowl, beat half-and-half cream and blend cheese until smooth. Add eggs and beat for 4 minutes until both mix well. Mix by hand and add cheese, garlic, salt, black pepper and Worcestershire sauce.

Combine breadcrumbs and butter and add to cheese mixture. Fold in vegetables. Pour into sprayed 9-inch spring form pan and bake for 55 minutes to 1 hour or until light brown and set in center.

Set out of oven for 10 minutes before slicing to serve. Be sure to use a knife to cut around edge of spring form pan before you open pan.

Spicy Vegetable Couscous

This is not only really good but is also a colorful dish!

1 (5.7 ounce) package herbed chicken couscous
3 tablespoons butter
3 tablespoons oil
1 small yellow squash, diced
1 small zucchini, diced
½ red onion, diced
1 red bell pepper, diced
1 (10 ounce) package frozen green peas, thawed
½ teaspoon garlic powder
½ teaspoon ground cumin
½ teaspoon curry powder
½ teaspoon red or cayenne pepper
½ teaspoon salt
½ teaspoon seasoned salt
1 cup shredded mozzarella cheese

Preheat oven to 350°. Cook couscous according to package directions, except add 3 tablespoons butter instead of specified amount.

In large skilled, heat oil and saute squash, zucchini, onion and bell pepper for 10 minutes but do not brown. Add peas, garlic powder, cumin, curry powder, red pepper, salt and seasoned salt and toss.

Combine vegetables and couscous. (If it seems a little dry, add few tablespoons of water.) Pour into sprayed 2-quart or 9 x 13-inch baking dish and sprinkle with mozzarella cheese.

Chill and heat later if you prefer. Set out of refrigerator for about 1 hour and then heat for 20 minutes. Serves 10 to 12.

Tip: If you don't like it HOT-HOT use only ¼ teaspoon red pepper.

Black-Eyed Peas and Tomatoes

1 bell pepper, chopped
1 large onion, chopped
2 ribs celery, chopped
2 tablespoons (¼ stick) butter
2 cans jalapeno black-eyed peas
1 (15 ounce) can stewed tomatoes
1 teaspoon garlic powder
¼ cup ketchup
2 teaspoons dry chicken broth

Sauté bell pepper, onion and celery in butter but do not overcook. (They should be a little crispy.) Add black-eyed peas, stewed tomatoes, garlic powder, ketchup and chicken broth.

Bring mixture to boil, reduce heat and simmer 10 minutes. Serves 8.

Worth-It Scalloped Potatoes

6 medium potatoes
½ cup (1 stick) butter
Black pepper
1 tablespoon flour
2 cups grated cheddar cheese
¾ cup milk

Preheat oven to 350°. Peel and wash potatoes. Slice half potatoes and place in 3-quart sprayed baking dish. Slice butter and place half butter over potatoes. Sprinkle with pepper, then flour and cover with half cheese.

Slice remaining potatoes, place over first layers and add remaining butter slices. Pour milk over dish and sprinkle a little more pepper.

Scatter remaining cheese over top, cover and bake for 1 hour. Cook immediately or potatoes will darken. It may be frozen after baking and then reheated. Serves 8.

The Ultimate Potato
Don't count the calories here!

6 large baking potatoes, peeled, boiled
1 cup light cream
5 tablespoons butter, melted
1 (8 ounce) package grated cheddar cheese
1 cup sour cream
½ cup chopped green onions
6 strips bacon, fried, crumbled

Preheat oven to 350°. Cool boiled potatoes and grate. Combine cream, butter, cheese and sour cream in double boiler and stir just until it melts.

(Continued on next page.)

(Continued)

Add cheese mixture to grated potatoes and place in sprayed baking dish. Bake for 30 minutes. Cover with onions and bacon and bake for another 5 minutes. Serves 8.

The Best Sweet Potato Casserole

1 (29 ounce) can sweet potatoes, drained
⅓ cup evaporated milk
¾ cup sugar
2 eggs, beaten
¼ cup (½ stick) butter, melted
1 teaspoon vanilla

Topping:

1 cup packed light brown sugar
⅓ cup (⅔ stick) butter, melted
½ cup flour
1 cup chopped pecans

Preheat oven to 350°. Place sweet potatoes in mixing bowl and mash slightly with fork. Add evaporated milk, sugar, eggs, butter and vanilla and mix well. Pour mixture into sprayed 7 x 11-inch baking dish.

Mix topping ingredients and sprinkle over top of casserole. Bake uncovered for 35 minutes or until crusty on top. Serves 8.

Red and Green Wild Rice

1 (6 ounce) package long grain and wild rice
3 carrots, peeled, cut into julienne strips
2 small zucchini, sliced
1 stalk fresh broccoli, cut into bite-size pieces
1 head cauliflower, cut into bite-size pieces
¼ cup (½ stick) butter, melted
Salt
1 teaspoon seasoned salt
½ cup toasted almonds
2 cups grated cheddar cheese

Preheat oven to 350°. Cook rice according to package directions and set aside. In large bowl, place carrots, zucchini, broccoli and cauliflower. Cover with wax paper and microwave for 3 minutes. Turn bowl and stir vegetables. Microwave for 2½ more minutes.

Add melted butter, few sprinkles of salt, seasoned salt, almonds and rice and toss. Pour into sprayed 9 x 13-inch glass baking dish. Bake covered for 10 to 15 minutes.

Sprinkle with cheese and return to oven for 5 minutes. Serves 8 to 10.

Hot Pasta Frittata

½ cup chopped onion
1 green bell pepper, chopped
1 red bell pepper, chopped
3 tablespoons butter
1 (7 ounce) box thin spaghetti, slightly broken up, cooked
1½ cup shredded mozzarella cheese
5 eggs
½ milk
⅓ cup grated parmesan cheese
1 tablespoon basil
1 teaspoon oregano
1 teaspoon salt
½ teaspoon white pepper

Preheat oven to 375°. In skillet over medium heat, sauté onion and bell peppers in butter for 5 minutes, but do not brown.

In large bowl combine onion-pepper mixture and spaghetti and toss. Add mozzarella cheese and toss.

In separate bowl, beat eggs, milk, parmesan cheese, basil, oregano, salt and pepper. Add spaghetti mixture and pour into buttered 9 x 13-inch baking pan (or 2-quart casserole baking dish).

Cover with foil and bake for 10 minutes. Uncover to make sure eggs are set. If not, then bake for 2 to 3 minutes longer. Cut into squares. Serves 8.

Tip: This can be prepared, chilled and baked later. Let it get to room temperature before placing in oven.

Carnival Couscous

This side dish is a rainbow of colors – delightful looking as well as delicious!

1 (6 ounce) package herbed chicken-flavor couscous with
   seasonings
1¼ cups water
5 tablespoons butter, divided
1 cup chopped red bell pepper
1 cup chopped green bell pepper
¾ cup coarsely shredded carrots
1 bunch green onions with tops, chopped
8 small fresh mushrooms, thinly sliced, optional
½ teaspoon garlic powder
1 teaspoon dried dill weed
½ teaspoon salt
½ teaspoon seasoned salt
½ teaspoon black pepper

In large saucepan, cook couscous with water, butter and seasoning packet according to package directions.

In skillet, place 3 tablespoons butter, bell peppers, carrots, onions and mushrooms and cook on medium heat 8 to 10 minutes. Add garlic, dill weed, salt, seasoned salt and black pepper. Add pepper-carrot mixture with couscous. (If couscous seems a little too dry, add on 2 tablespoons of water.)

Serve immediately or place in baking dish and warm at 300° for about 20 minutes. (This is really better when you serve it the same day you make it without being chilled.) Serves 6 to 8.

Fettuccine Supreme

1 (8 ounce) package fettuccine
½ cup whipping cream
½ cup (1 stick) butter, sliced
½ teaspoon dried basil
1 tablespoon dried parsley
¼ teaspoon pepper
¼ teaspoon salt, optional
1 cup grated parmesan cheese

Cook fettuccine according to package directions and drain.
Immediately place fettuccine back into saucepan, add
whipping cream, butter, basil, parsley and pepper.

Toss until butter melts. Fold in parmesan cheese, pour
into serving bowl and serve hot. Serves 8.

Extreme Cheddar-Potato Casserole
This is a "winner" for the easiest and best potato dish!

1 (2 pound) bag frozen hash brown potatoes, thawed
1 onion, finely chopped
¾ cup (1½ sticks) butter, melted, divided
1 cup sour cream
1 (10 ounce) can cream of chicken soup
2 cups grated cheddar cheese
1½ cups corn flakes, crushed

Preheat oven to 350°. In large bowl, combine hash
browns, onion, ½ cup (1 stick) butter, sour cream, soup
and cheese and mix well.

Pour into sprayed 9 x 13-inch baking dish. Combine corn
flakes and ¼ cup (½ stick) butter, sprinkle over mixture
and bake for 45 minutes.

Creamy Macaroni and Cheese

1 (12 ounce) package macaroni pasta
⅓ cup (⅔ stick) butter
¼ cup flour
2 cups milk
1 (16 ounce) carton cubed, processed cheese
1 teaspoon salt
½ teaspoon white pepper

Preheat oven to 350°. Cook macaroni according to package directions, drain and set aside. Melt butter in saucepan and stir in flour until it blends well. Add milk and stir mixture constantly until thick. Add cheese and stir until it melts.

Add cheese sauce to macaroni and combine well. Pour into sprayed 2½-quart baking dish and bake for 30 minutes or until bubbly. Serves 10.

Three-Cheese Manicotti

1½ cups water
1 (8 ounce) can tomato sauce
1 (1½ ounce) package spaghetti sauce mix
2½ cups grated mozzarella cheese, divided
1 cup ricotta or small-curd cottage cheese
½ cup grated parmesan cheese
2 eggs, beaten
½ teaspoon salt
¼ teaspoon pepper
8 manicotti shells

Preheat oven to 350°. Combine water, tomato sauce
and spaghetti sauce mix in small saucepan. Simmer
uncovered for 10 minutes.

In mixing bowl, combine 1 cup mozzarella cheese, ricotta,
parmesan, eggs, salt and pepper, stir gently and set aside.

Cook manicotti shells according to package directions and
drain. Stuff ¼ cup cheese mixture into manicotti shells.

Pour ½ cup sauce into 9 x 13-inch baking dish and
arrange manicotti shells in sauce. Pour remaining sauce
over top. Sprinkle with remaining mozzarella cheese.
Bake uncovered for 30 minutes or until bubbly. Serves 4.

Cornbread Dressing and Gravy

2 (6 ounce) packages cornbread mix
9 biscuits or 1 biscuit mix recipe
1 small onion, chopped
2 ribs celery, chopped
2 eggs
Black pepper
2 teaspoons poultry seasoning
3 (15 ounce) cans chicken broth

Gravy:

2 (15 ounce) cans chicken broth
2 heaping tablespoons cornstarch
Black pepper
2 hard-boiled eggs, sliced, optional

Preheat oven to 350°. Prepare cornbread and biscuits according to package directions in advance of making recipe.

Crumble cornbread and biscuits into large bowl and use a little more cornbread than biscuits. Add onion, celery, eggs and seasonings and stir in 2½ cans broth. If mixture is not "runny", add remaining broth. If still not runny, add a little milk.

Bake in sprayed 9 x 13-inch baking dish for 45 minutes or until golden brown. This may be frozen uncooked but thaw before cooking.

For gravy, combine ½ cup broth with cornstarch and mix until there are no lumps. Add remaining broth and heat to boil. Stir constantly until broth is thick. Add boiled eggs.

Main Dishes

Chili-Relleno Hit

1 pound lean ground beef
1 bell pepper, chopped
1 onion, chopped
1 (4 ounce) can chopped green chilies, drained
1 teaspoon oregano
1 teaspoon dried cilantro leaves
½ teaspoon garlic powder
½ teaspoon salt
½ teaspoon pepper
1 (7 ounce) can whole green chilies, drained
1½ cups grated Monterey Jack cheese
1½ cups sharp cheddar cheese
3 large eggs
1 tablespoon flour
1 cup half-and-half cream

Preheat oven to 350°. In skillet, brown meat with bell pepper, onion, chopped green chilies, oregano, cilantro, garlic powder, salt and pepper. Seed whole chili peppers and spread on bottom of sprayed 9 x 13-inch baking dish.

Cover with meat mixture and sprinkle with cheeses. Combine eggs and flour and beat with fork until fluffy. Add half-and-half cream, mix well and pour over top of meat in baking dish. Bake for 30 to 35 minutes or until light brown.

Tip: You could use the chopped green chilies instead of the whole green chilies.

Marvelous Meat Loaf

1 pound ground turkey
1 pound ground beef
2 eggs
1 (1 ounce) package dry onion soup mix
¼ cup ketchup
¼ cup minced bell pepper
½ cup sour cream
½ teaspoon garlic powder
½ teaspoon pepper
2 teaspoons Worcestershire sauce
1 cup crushed crackers

Topping:

1¼ cups ketchup
1 cup packed brown sugar
3 tablespoons Dijon mustard
Several shakes hot sauce

In large mixing bowl, combine all meat loaf ingredients and mix well.

Place meat mixture in sprayed 9 x 13-inch baking pan and shape into loaf. (Load should be bout size of loaf pan but with rounded corners.) Cook for 1 hour.

While meat cooks, combine topping ingredients in medium saucepan and heat. Pour topping for meat loaf separately in gravy boat. Serves 8.

Super Spaghetti Pie

6 ounces cooked, drained spaghetti
⅓ cup grated parmesan cheese
1 egg, beaten
1 tablespoon butter, melted
1 cup small-curd cottage cheese
½ pound ground beef
½ pound ground pork sausage
½ cup chopped onion
1 (15 ounce) can tomato sauce
1 teaspoon garlic powder
1 tablespoon sugar
½ teaspoon salt
½ teaspoon seasoned pepper
1 teaspoon oregano
½ cup mozzarella cheese

Preheat oven to 350°. While spaghetti is still warm, combine with parmesan cheese, egg and butter in large bowl. Pour into sprayed 10-inch pie plate and pat mixture up and around sides with spoon to form crust. Put cottage cheese over spaghetti layer.

In skillet, brown ground meat, sausage and onion. Drain fat, add tomato sauce and seasonings and simmer for 10 minutes.

Spoon meat mixture on top of cottage cheese and bake for 30 minutes. Arrange mozzarella on top and return to oven until cheese melts. Serves 8.

Tip: *This may be made in advance and placed in refrigerator until ready to cook.*

Smash Hit Steak Casserole

2 pounds lean round steak, tenderized
Seasoned salt
Seasoned pepper
2 tablespoons oil
1 onion, chopped
1 cup uncooked rice
1 (15 ounce) can beef broth
1 (15 ounce) can water plus ¼ cup
2 tablespoons Worcestershire sauce
1 bell pepper, chopped
1 (4 ounce) can chopped green chilies, optional
1 (2 ounce) jar sliced pimento, drained

Preheat oven to 350°. Trim fat off edges of steak, cut into serving-size pieces and season with seasoned salt and pepper. Pour oil into large, 12-inch skillet. (It must hold at least 3 quarts.)

In skillet, brown steak on both sides. Combine onion, rice, beef broth, water, Worcestershire sauce, bell pepper, green chilies and pimento and pour over steak. Stir slightly to mix ingredients. Bring mixture to boil.

Reduce heat to low simmer, cover and simmer covered for 35 minutes. Serves 8.

Swiss Steak Supper

1 to 1½ pounds well-trimmed, boneless round steak,
   tenderized
Salt and pepper
Flour
Oil
2 onions, chopped
5 carrots, sliced
¾ teaspoon garlic powder
1 (16 ounce) can tomatoes, coarsely chopped
¾ cup picante sauce
½ cup water
2 teaspoons instant beef bouillon
1 tablespoon dried cilantro
1 teaspoon salt

Preheat oven to 325°. Cut meat into serving-size pieces
and sprinkle with salt and pepper. Dredge in flour and coat
well.

Heat oil in large skillet and brown meat on both sides.
Remove steak to 9 x 13-inch baking dish and cover with
onions and carrots.

Use same skillet to combine garlic, tomatoes, picante
sauce, water, beef bouillon, cilantro and salt. Heat and stir
just to boiling point.

Pour mixture over steak, onions and carrots. Cook
covered for 1 hour. Serves 8.

Tip: This dish may be made in advance and reheated just
      before serving.

Lone Star Chicken-Fried Steak and Gravy

2 pounds round steak, tenderized
1¼ cups flour
1 teaspoon salt
Seasoned pepper
2 eggs, slightly beaten
½ cup milk
Oil

Cream Gravy:

6 to 8 tablespoons pan grease or bacon drippings
6 tablespoons flour
3 cups milk
½ teaspoon salt
¼ teaspoon pepper

Trim steak and cut into 6 to 8 pieces. Combine flour, salt and pepper and dredge steak pieces in flour mixture and coat well. In separate bowl, combine eggs and milk.

Dip steak into egg mixture and dredge again in flour to enough flour mashed into steak. Heat ½-inch oil in heavy skillet and fry steak until golden brown.

To make gravy, remove steaks to warm oven, retain drippings (bacon drippings make better gravy if you have some) and add flour. Cook and stir until flour begins to brown. Add milk and stir until mixture is thick. Season mixture with salt and pepper and serve in separate gravy bowl.

Mom's Best Pot Roast

1 (4 to 5 pound) boneless rump roast
Seasoned salt
Seasoned pepper
Garlic powder
2 cups water
6 medium potatoes, peeled, quartered
8 carrots, peeled, quartered
3 onions, peeled, quartered

Gravy:

3 tablespoons cornstarch
¾ cup water
½ teaspoon salt
½ teaspoon pepper

Preheat oven to 375°. Set roast in roasting pan with lid and sprinkle liberally with salt, pepper and garlic powder. Add 2 cups water and cook for 30 minutes.

Reduce heat to 325° and cook for 3 hours. Add potatoes, carrots and onions and cook another 35 to 40 minutes. Lift roast out of pan, move to serving platter and place potatoes, carrots and onion around roast.

To make gravy, combine cornstarch and water and add to juices remaining in roaster. Add salt and pepper. While on stovetop, cook on HIGH and stir constantly until gravy is thick. Serve in gravy boat with roast and vegetables. Serves 8.

Savory Oven-Herb Chicken

2 cups crushed corn flakes
½ cup grated parmesan cheese
1 tablespoon rosemary
1 tablespoon thyme leaves
1 teaspoon oregano
1 tablespoon parsley flakes
½ teaspoon garlic powder
½ teaspoon salt
1 teaspoon black pepper
8 boneless, skinless chicken breast halves or 1 chicken,
   quartered
½ cup (1 stick) butter, melted

Preheat oven to 325°. In medium bowl, mix corn flakes, parmesan cheese, rosemary, thyme, oregano, parsley, garlic powder, salt and pepper.

Place butter in small bowl and melt in microwave. Dip chicken breasts in butter and corn flake mixture and coat well.

Place in sprayed, shallow 9 x 13-inch baking dish. Do not crowd pieces. Bake uncovered for 1 hour.

Three-Cheers Chicken

8 boneless, skinless chicken breast halves
Salt and pepper
6 tablespoons (¾ stick) butter
1 onion, chopped
½ bell pepper, chopped
1 (4 ounce) jar chopped pimentos, drained
1 cup uncooked rice
1 (10 ounce) can cream of chicken soup
1 (10 ounce) can cream of celery soup
2 soup cans water
1 (8 ounce) can sliced water chestnuts
1 cup grated cheddar cheese

Preheat oven to 350°. Salt and pepper chicken and place in large 11 x 14-inch glass baking dish. Melt butter and add onion, bell pepper, pimentos, rice, soups, water and water chestnuts and pour over chicken.

Bake for 15 minutes, reduce oven temperature to 325° and cook for 1 hour more. Add cheese 5 minutes before dish is done and return to oven for last 5 minutes.

Aloha Chicken

2 medium-sized chickens, skinned, quartered
Salt and pepper
Flour
Oil
1 (20 ounce) can sliced pineapple
1 cup sugar
3 tablespoons cornstarch
¾ cup vinegar
1 tablespoon soy sauce
¼ teaspoon ginger
2 chicken bouillon cubes
1 tablespoon lemon juice
2 bell peppers, julienned
Cooked rice

Preheat oven to 350°. Wash chicken and pat dry with
paper towel. Rub and coat chicken with salt, pepper and
flour. Brown chicken quarters in oil and place in large,
shallow roasting pan.

To make sauce, drain pineapple by pouring syrup into
2-cup measure. Add water or orange juice to make
1½ cups. In medium saucepan, combine sugar,
cornstarch, pineapple syrup, vinegar, soy sauce, ginger,
bouillon cubes and lemon juice and bring to boil. Stir
mixture for 2 minutes or until thick and clear and pour over
browned chicken.

Bake covered for 40 minutes. Place pineapple slices and
bell pepper on top of chicken and bake 10 to 15 minutes
longer. Serve on fluffy white rice. Serves 8.

Succulent Pecan-Chicken Breasts

⅓ cup (⅔ stick) butter
1 cup flour
1 cup finely ground pecans
¼ cup sesame seeds
1 tablespoon paprika
1 teaspoon salt
¼ teaspoon pepper
¼ egg, beaten
1 cup buttermilk
6 large or 8 small boneless, skinless chicken breast
  halves
⅓ cup coarsely chopped pecans

Preheat oven to 350°. Melt butter in large 9 x 13-inch baking dish and set aside. Combine flour, finely ground pecans, sesame seeds, paprika, salt and pepper.

Combine egg and buttermilk in separate bowl. Dip chicken in egg mixture, dredge in flour mixture and coat well.

Place chicken in baking dish and turn once to coat with butter. Sprinkle with chopped pecans. Bake for 40 minutes or until golden brown. Garnish with fresh parsley or sage.

Tip: Chicken may be cut into strips, prepared the same way and used as an appetizer. A honey-mustard dressing would be nice for dipping. This recipe could also be used for fish, like orange roughy, if cooking time is reduced in half.

Speedy Chicken and Tortilla Dumplings

6 large boneless, skinless chicken breast halves
9 to 10 cups water
2 ribs celery, chopped
1 small onion, chopped
About 2 tablespoons chicken broth
1 (10 ounce) can cream of chicken soup, undiluted
10 or 11 (8-inch) flour tortillas

In large roaster, place chicken breasts and enough water to cover celery and onion. Bring to boil, reduce heat and cook for 30 minutes or until chicken is tender.

Remove chicken and reserve broth in roaster. (You should have 8 to 9 cups of broth.) Let chicken cool and cut into bite-size pieces. Gradually add broth. Taste to make sure broth is rich and tasty. Add chicken soup and bring to boil.

Cut tortillas into 2 (1-inch) strips. Add strips, one at a time, to briskly boiling broth mixture and stir constantly. Add chicken, reduce heat and simmer for 5 to 10 minutes. Stir often to prevent dumplings from sticking. Serves 8.

Chicken Souffle Supreme

16 slices white bread
6 boneless, skinless chicken breast halves, cooked
½ cup mayonnaise
1 cup grated cheddar cheese, divided
5 large eggs
2 cups milk
1 teaspoon salt
1 (10 ounce) can cream of mushroom soup

Preheat oven to 350°. Butter bread slices on 1 side and remove crusts.

Butter 9 x 13-inch baking dish and line 8 bread slices in bottom of dish. Cover with chicken, spread mayonnaise and sprinkle ½ cup cheese. (You could use deli-sliced chicken instead of cooking chicken breasts.)

Top with remaining 8 slices bread. Beat eggs, milk and salt and pour over entire dish. Chill overnight or all day.

When ready to bake, spread soup over top and press down with back of spoon. Bake covered for 45 minutes.

Uncover, sprinkle with remaining ½ cup cheddar cheese return to oven and bake for 15 minutes longer. Serves 8 to 10.

South-of-the-Border Chicken

8 boneless, skinless chicken breast halves
1 cup grated Monterey Jack cheese
½ cup grated cheddar cheese
1 (4 ounce) can chopped green chilies, drained
1 teaspoon cilantro
3 tablespoons onion flakes
⅓ cup (⅔ stick) butter
2 teaspoons cumin
1 teaspoon chili powder
Tortilla chips, crushed

Preheat oven to 350°. Pound chicken breasts to about ¼-inch thickness. In bowl, mix cheeses, chilies, cilantro and onion.

Place 2 to 3 tablespoons cheese mixture on each chicken breast and roll up and place seam side down in sprayed baking dish. In saucepan, melt butter, add cumin and chili powder and pour over chicken.

Bake covered for 45 minutes, uncover and top with crushed chips. Return to oven and bake for 3 more minutes.

Chicken Pepe

Oil
3 onions, chopped
3 bell peppers, chopped
1 teaspoon garlic powder
2 (10 ounce) cans tomatoes and chilies
1 (16 ounce) package cubed, processed cheese
1 (16 ounce) package shredded cheddar cheese
6 cups chopped, cooked chicken
1 (16 ounce) carton sour cream
1 (3 ounce) jar pimentos, drained
Cooked rice
Small corn chips

Cook onion, bell pepper and garlic in a little oil. Add tomatoes and green chilies and bring to boil. Reduce heat and simmer 15 minutes or until thick.

Add cheeses and heat slowly until cheese melts. Add chicken, sour cream and pimentos.
Heat well but do not boil.

Serve over layer of rice and layer of small corn chips.
Serves 12.

Chicken Fiesta

½ cup (1 stick) butter
2 cups finely crushed cheese crackers
2 tablespoons taco seasoning mix
8 boneless, skinless chicken breast halves
1 bunch green onions with tops, chopped
1 teaspoon chicken bouillon
2 cups whipping cream
2 cups grated Monterey Jack cheese
1 (4 ounce) can chopped green chilies, drained

Preheat oven to 350°. Melt butter in 9 x 13-inch baking
dish and set aside.

Pound chicken breasts to ¼-inch thick. Combine cracker
crumbs and taco mix and dredge chicken in mixture.
Make sure crumbs stick to chicken.

Place chicken breasts in baking dish with butter. Take out
several tablespoons melted butter and place in saucepan.
Add onions and saute.

Turn off heat, add chicken bouillon and stir. Add whipping
cream, Monterey Jack cheese and chopped green chilies
and mix well. Pour over chicken in baking dish. Bake
uncovered for 55 minutes.

Old-Fashioned Chicken Spaghetti

8 to 10 ounces spaghetti
1 bell pepper, chopped
1 onion, chopped
1 cup chopped celery
½ cup (1 stick) butter
1 (10 ounce) can tomato soup
1 (10 ounce) can diced tomatoes and green chilies
1 (4 ounce) can chopped mushrooms
½ teaspoon salt
½ teaspoon pepper
½ teaspoon garlic powder
3 teaspoons chicken bouillon
½ cup water
4 to 5 cups chopped chicken or turkey
1 (8 ounce) package cubed, processed cheese
1 (8 ounce) package shredded cheddar cheese

Preheat oven to 325°. Cook spaghetti according to package directions and drain. In medium saucepan, saute bell pepper, onion and celery in butter. Add soup, tomatoes, mushrooms, salt, pepper, garlic powder, bouillon and water and mix.

In large mixing bowl, mix spaghetti, soup, tomato mixture, chicken and cheese. Place in 2 (2-quart) sprayed baking dishes. Bake one dish covered for 40 to 50 minutes. Freeze the other dish for later. To cook frozen dish, thaw first.

Tip: This is a good recipe for leftover turkey.

Creamy Turkey Enchiladas Extraordinaire

Forget about the calories. These enchiladas are worth it. They are one of my favorites.

2 tablespoons (¼ stick) butter
1 onion, finely chopped
3 green onions with tops, chopped
½ teaspoon garlic powder
½ teaspoon seasoned salt
1 (7 ounce) can chopped green chilies, drained
2 (8 ounce) packages cream cheese, softened
3 cups diced turkey or chicken
8 (8-inch) flour tortillas
2 (8 ounce) cartons whipping cream
1 (16 ounce) package shredded Monterey Jack cheese

Preheat oven to 350°. Add butter to large skillet and sauté onions. Add garlic powder, seasoned salt and green chilies and stir in cream cheese. Heat and stir until cream cheese melts. Add diced chicken.

Lay out 8 tortillas and spoon 3 heaping tablespoons turkey mixture on each tortilla. Roll up tortillas and place seam side down in large, lightly sprayed 9 x 13-inch baking dish.

Pour whipping cream over enchiladas, sprinkle cheese on top and bake uncovered for 35 minutes.

Apricot-Baked Ham

1 (12 to 20 pound) whole ham, fully cooked, bone-in
Whole cloves
2 tablespoons dry mustard
1¼ cups apricot jam
1¼ cups packed light brown sugar

Preheat oven to 450°. Trim skin and excess fat from ham.
Place ham on oven rack in large roasting pan and insert
cloves every inch or so. Be sure to push cloves into ham
surface as far as they will go.

Combine dry mustard and jam and spread over entire
surface of ham. Pat brown sugar over jam mixture, reduce
heat to 325° and bake uncovered at 15 minutes per pound.
Sugary crust that forms on ham keeps juices in.

When ham is done, remove from oven and set aside
20 minutes before carving.

Pineapple-Glazed Ham

7 to 9 pound butt-end ham, partially cooked
Whole cloves
1 (14 ounce) can chunk pineapple, reserve juice
Maraschino cherries, optional

Sauce:

1 cup red wine or cooking wine
1 cup packed brown sugar
Scant tablespoon cut-up crystallized ginger
1½ teaspoons Dijon mustard
1 (8 ounce) crushed pineapple

Preheat oven to 350°. Insert LOTS of whole cloves on outside of ham. Using toothpicks insert pineapple chunks into ham. Add cherry on top of pineapple chunk, if you like.

In saucepan, combine wine, brown sugar, crystallized ginger, mustard, crushed pineapple and juice from chunk pineapple and bring to a boil.

Turn off heat, place ham in roasting pan and pour hot sauce over ham. Cook at 10 to 15 minutes per pound and baste with sauce every 20 minutes.

Saucy Ham Loaf

1 pound ham, ground
½ pound ground beef
½ pound ground pork
2 eggs
1 cup bread or cracker crumbs
2 teaspoons Worcestershire sauce
1 (5 ounce) can evaporated milk
3 tablespoons chili sauce
1 teaspoon seasoned salt
1 teaspoon seasoned pepper
Bacon to strip top of loaf, optional

Sweet-and-Hot Mustard:

4 ounces dry mustard
1 cup vinegar
3 eggs, beaten
1 cup sugar

Preheat oven to 350°. Have butcher grind all 3 meats together. Combine all ingredients except bacon and mustard sauce ingredients.

Form into loaf in 9 x 13-inch baking pan. Place bacon strip over top and bake for 1 hour.

To prepare hot mustard, mix mustard and vinegar until smooth and set aside overnight. Add eggs and sugar and cook in double boiler. Stir for 8 to 10 minutes or until mixture coats spoon.

Cool and store in covered jars in refrigerator. Serve with ham loaf.

Tip: The hot mustard recipe also goes well on sandwiches.

Pork Loin with Apricot Glaze

1 (3½ to 4 pound) center-cut pork loin
1 tablespoon olive oil
Seasoned pepper
1 teaspoon dried rosemary
1 cup dry white wine or cooking wine
1 cup water
1½ cups apricot preserves

Preheat oven to 350°. Rub pork loin with olive oil and sprinkle seasoned pepper and rosemary over roast. Place loin in shallow roasting pan. Pour wine and water into pan and roast for 1 hour.

Remove pan from oven and spoon about 1 cup pan drippings into small bowl. Add apricot preserves and mix well. Pour mixture over pork, reduce oven to 325° and return to oven. Continue to roast for 1 hour more and baste 2 to 3 times with pan drippings.

Set aside pork for 15 minutes before slicing. (To cook day before, cook as directed and let roast cool.) Remove roast from drippings, place in glass baking dish and slice.

Pour drippings into separate container and chill both. When ready to serve, heat drippings and pour over roast. Warm in 350° oven for 20 minutes.

Sweet-and-Sour Pork Loin Roast

4 to 5 pound pork loin roast
Oil
Seasoned salt and pepper
½ cup water
1 (12 ounce) bottle chili sauce
1 (12 ounce) jar apricot preserves
1 (20 ounce) can chunk pineapple
2 bell peppers, sliced

Preheat oven to 350°. In Dutch oven roaster, brown roast in a little oil. Add seasoned salt and pepper and water to pan, cover and bake for 1 hour.

Mix chili sauce and apricot preserves and pour over roast. Reduce oven temperature to 250° and cook for 2 hours.

Add pineapple and bell pepper and cook another 15 minutes. Serves 8.

Perfect Grilled Pork Tenderloin

2 pork tenderloins

Marinade:

⅔ cup soy sauce
⅔ cup oil
2 heaping tablespoons crystallized ginger, finely chopped
2 tablespoons real lime juice
1 teaspoon garlic powder
2 tablespoons minced onion

Combine all marinade ingredients in large, resealable plastic bag. Add pork tenderloins and marinate for 24 to 36 hours.

(Continued on next page.)

(Continued)

When ready to serve, cook over charcoal for 45 minutes. Baste occasionally with remaining marinade. Serves 6 to 8.

Blackened Fish Filets

3 teaspoons paprika
1 teaspoon garlic powder
1 teaspoon onion powder
2 teaspoon salt
1 teaspoon crushed red pepper
1 teaspoon white pepper
1 teaspoon black pepper
½ teaspoon thyme
½ teaspoon oregano
4 (¼-inch thick) fish filets
½ cup (1 stick) butter, melted

On wax paper square, mix paprika, garlic and onion powder, salt, red pepper, white pepper, black pepper, thyme and oregano. (This is blackening mixture.)

Brush fish filets on both sides with melted butter. Generously sprinkle fish with blackened mixture and coat both sides well.

Heat large cast-iron skillet over very high heat until it is beyond smoking stage. (Skillet cannot be too hot for this dish.) Place 1 tablespoon butter in skillet and blackened filet in hot skillet. Add 1 teaspoon melted butter on top of each filet and cook for 2 minutes per side.

Serve immediately.

Old-Fashioned Salmon Croquettes

1 (15 ounce) can salmon
½ teaspoon seasoned salt
½ teaspoon black pepper
¼ cup shrimp cocktail sauce or chili sauce
½ (10 ounce) can cream of chicken soup
1 egg
½ onion, finely chopped
Several dashes hot sauce
1⅓ cups cracker crumbs
Flour
Oil

Drain salmon well in colander and remove skin and little back bones. In mixing bowl, add salmon, seasoned salt, pepper, cocktail sauce, soup, egg, onion, hot sauce and cracker crumbs and mix well.

Pat croquettes into shapes like triangle-shaped log and roll in flour. Make about 10 to 12 logs.

Pour just enough oil in bottom of large skillet, add croquettes and fry on medium heat. Turn twice so you have 3 sides that brown. (Add extra tablespoon oil halfway through cooking if needed.) It will take about 15 minutes to fry on 3 sides. (Of course, you could deep-fry croquettes if you want.)

Tip: Use remaining cream of chicken soup by diluting with equal parts of milk and have cup of soup as an appetizer.

Tequila-Lime Shrimp

¼ cup (½ stick) butter
2 tablespoons olive oil
½ teaspoon garlic powder
1½ pounds medium shrimp, shelled, veined
3 tablespoons tequila
3 tablespoons lime juice
½ teaspoon salt
½ teaspoon chili powder
¼ teaspoon seasoned salt
¼ teaspoon black pepper
½ teaspoon ground coriander
1 tablespoon dried cilantro
Hot, cooked rice

Pat shrimp dry with paper towel. In large skillet, heat butter and oil over medium heat. Add garlic powder and shrimp and cook for 2 minutes. Stir occasionally.

Add in tequila, lime juice, salt, chili powder, seasoned salt, pepper and coriander. Cook for 2 minutes more (most of liquid will be gone and shrimp should be pink and glazed.) Add cilantro.

Serve over hot, cooked rice.

Angel-Crab Pasta

½ cup (1 stick) butter
½ onion, finely chopped
1 bell pepper, chopped
1 teaspoon dried summer savory
1 teaspoon dried parsley flakes
1 teaspoon dried basil
½ teaspoon celery salt
1 teaspoon lemon pepper
½ teaspoon salt
2 (16 ounce) cans diced tomato
1 (16 ounce) can Italian-style stewed tomatoes
½ cup dry white wine, optional
1 pound crabmeat or lobster
1 pound angel hair pasta, cooked
Freshly grated parmesan cheese

In large saucepan, melt butter and saute onion and bell pepper. Stir in all seasonings and tomatoes and bring to a boil. Add wine and simmer for 5 minutes. Add crabmeat and simmer for 2 minutes.

Place warm pasta in serving dish and top with crab mixture. Serve with parmesan cheese. Serves 6 to 8.

Desserts

Hot Apricot Cobbler

A bridge partner had this recently and everybody gave this a "blue ribbon". This is another one of those recipes that is really quick and easy plus really delicious.

1 (20 ounce) can apricot pie filling
1 (20 ounce) can crushed pineapple, with juice
1 cup chopped pecans
1 (18 ounce) box yellow cake mix
1 cup (2 sticks) butter, melted
Whipped topping

Preheat oven to 375°. Pour apricot pie filling into sprayed 9 x 13-inch baking dish and spread out. Spoon crushed pineapple and juice over pie filling. Sprinkle pecans over pineapple then sprinkle cake mix over pecans.

Pour melted butter over cake mix and bake for 40 minutes or until light brown and crunchy. To serve, top with whipped topping. Serves 10.

Celebration Kahula Pie

26 marshmallows
1 (13 ounce) can evaporated milk
1 (1 ounce) package unflavored gelatin
¼ cup cold water
1 (8 ounce) carton whipping cream
½ cup kahula
1 (9-inch) chocolate cookie piecrust
Chocolate curls

In saucepan over low to medium heat, melt marshmallows with evaporated milk. Stir constantly and do not let milk boil.

Remove from heat and add gelatin that has been dissolved in cold water. Chill until mixture is slightly thick.

(Continued on next page.)

(Continued)

Whip cream and fold into marshmallow mixture. Mix in kahula and pour into piecrust. Garnish with chocolate and curls and chill overnight.

Outa-Sight Pie

1 (14 ounce) can sweetened, condensed milk
1 (20 ounce) can lemon pie filling
1 (20 ounce) can crushed pineapple, drained
1 (8 ounce) carton whipped topping
2 (9-inch) cookie-flavored ready piecrusts

In large mixing bowl, combine condensed milk, lemon pie filling and pineapple and mix well. Fold in whipped topping and pour mixture into 2 piecrusts.

Chill several hours before serving.

Creamy Lemon Pie

1 (8 ounce) package cream cheese, softened
1 (14 ounce) can sweetened, condensed milk
¼ cup lemon juice
1 (20 ounce) can lemon pie filling
1 (9-inch) graham cracker piecrust

In mixing bowl, cream cheese until smooth and creamy. Add condensed milk and lemon juice and beat until mixture is creamy.

Fold in lemon pie filling and stir well. Pour into piecrust and chill several hours before slicing and serving.

Peach-Mousse Pie

1 (9-inch) graham cracker piecrust
1 (16 ounce) package frozen peach slices, thawed
1 cup sugar
1 (1 ounce) package unflavored gelatin
⅛ teaspoon ground nutmeg
A few drops yellow and red food coloring
1 (12 ounce) carton whipped topping
Nectarine slices for garnish

Place peaches in blender and process until peaches
are smooth. Pour into saucepan, bring to boil and stir
constantly. Remove from burner.

Combine sugar, gelatin and nutmeg and stir into hot puree
until sugar and gelatin dissolve. Pour gelatin mixture into
large bowl and place in freezer for 20 minutes or until
mixture mounds. Stir occasionally.

Using mixer, beat mixture on HIGH speed for 5 minutes or
until light and fluffy. Add coloring, fold in whipped topping
and pour into piecrust.

Birthday Pumpkin-Chiffon Pie
The best pumpkin pie you'll ever eat!

1 (1 ounce) package unflavored gelatin
¼ cup cold water
2 eggs
1¼ cups sugar
1¼ cups canned pumpkin
⅔ cup milk
½ teaspoon ground ginger
½ teaspoon nutmeg
⅓ teaspoon cinnamon
½ teaspoon salt
1 (8 ounce) carton whipping cream
1 (9-inch) baked piecrust

Soften gelatin in cold water and set aside. Using mixer, beat eggs for 3 minutes. Add sugar, pumpkin, milk, spices and salt and mix well.

Pour mixture into large saucepan, cook in double boiler and stir constantly until mixture reaches custard consistency. Mix in softened gelatin, dissolve in hot pumpkin mixture and cool.

When mixture is cool, whip cream until very stiff and fold into pumpkin mixture. (Do not use whipped topping.) Pour into piecrust and chill several hours before slicing.

Tip: *Original "chiffon" pies had egg whites whipped and folded into pie. Because raw eggs are not good in uncooked recipes, this recipe cooks the whole eggs and adds whipped cream. It is delicious!*

Easy Pineapple Cake

2 cups sugar
2 cups flour
1 (20 ounce) can crushed pineapple, with juice
1 teaspoon baking soda
½ teaspoon salt
1 teaspoon vanilla

Icing:

1 (8 ounce) package cream cheese, softened
½ cup (1 stick) butter, melted
1 cup powdered sugar
1 cup chopped pecans

Preheat oven to 350°. Combine all cake ingredients and mix well by hand. Pour into sprayed 9 x 13-inch baking pan and bake for 30 to 35 minutes.

To prepare icing, beat all ingredients except pecans with mixer. Add pecans, stir to mix well and spread icing over hot cake.

The Best Fresh Apple Cake

1½ cups oil
2 cups sugar
3 eggs
2½ cups sifted flour
½ teaspoon salt
1 teaspoon baking soda
2 teaspoons baking powder
½ teaspoon cinnamon
1 teaspoon vanilla
3 cups peeled, grated apples
1 cup chopped pecans

Glaze:

2 tablespoons (¼ stick) butter, melted
2 tablespoons milk
1 cup powdered sugar
1 teaspoon vanilla
¼ teaspoon lemon extract

Preheat oven to 350°. Spray tube pan. Mix oil, sugar and eggs and beat well.

In separate bowl, sift flour, salt, baking soda, baking powder and cinnamon. Gradually add flour mixture to cream mixture. Add vanilla and fold in apples and pecans and pour into prepared tube pan. Bake for 1 hour.

Remove from oven, cool and invert onto serving plate.

For glaze, combine and mix all ingredients and drizzle over cake.

Sweet Orange-Date Cake

4 cups flour
1 teaspoon baking soda
1 cup (2 sticks) butter, softened
2½ cups sugar
4 eggs
1½ cups buttermilk
1 teaspoon orange extract
1 tablespoon grated orange rind
1 (11 ounce) can mandarin oranges
1 (8 ounce) package chopped dates
1 cup chopped pecans

Glaze:

½ cup orange juice
1¼ cups sugar
1 teaspoon orange rind
½ teaspoon orange extract

Preheat oven to 350°. Sift flour and baking soda and set
aside. Cream butter and sugar, add eggs one at a time and
beat well. Add buttermilk and dry ingredients alternately
and end with dry ingredients. Add orange extract and rind
and beat well. Stir in oranges, dates and pecans.

Pour into sprayed bundt pan and bake for 1 hour,
15 minutes or until cake tests done. Remove from oven
and pour glaze over cake while still in pan.

To make glaze, mix orange juice, sugar, orange rind and
extract. Bring to a boil and then cool. Pour glaze slowly
over cake.

*Tip: If you don't happen to have buttermilk on hand just put
2 tablespoons lemon juice in 1½ cups milk and set aside
for 10 or 15 minutes. Presto, you'll have buttermilk.*

Christmas Lemon-Pecan Cake

1 (1.5 ounce) bottle lemon extract
4 cups pecan halves
2 cups (4 sticks) butter
3 cups sugar
3½ cups flour, divided
6 eggs
½ pound candied green pineapple, chopped
½ pound candied red cherries, halved
1½ teaspoons baking powder
½ cup flour

Preheat oven to 275°. Pour lemon extract over pecans in medium bowl, toss and set aside. Spray tube cake pan.

In large mixing bowl, cream butter and sugar until fluffy. Sift 3 cups flour and baking powder in separate bowl. Add eggs to butter-sugar mixture, one at a time, alternating with flour mixture.

With pineapple and cherries cut, add ½ cup flour and mix to coat well with flour. Fold in fruit and pecans and pour into tube pan.

Bake for 2 hours, 30 minutes or until done. Cool and remove carefully from pan.

Chocolate Hurricane Cake

This is easy and very, very yummy.

1 cup chopped pecans
1 (3 ounce) can sweetened flaked coconut
1 (18 ounce) box German chocolate cake mix
1¼ cups water
⅓ cup oil
3 eggs
½ cup (1 stick) butter, melted
1 (8 ounce) package cream cheese, softened
1 (16 ounce) box powdered sugar

Preheat oven to 350°. Spray 9 x 13-inch baking pan. Cover bottom of pan with pecans and coconut.

In mixing bowl, combine cake mix, water, oil and eggs and beat well. Carefully pour batter over pecans and coconut.

In mixing bowl, combine butter, cream cheese and powdered sugar and whip to blend. Spoon mixture over unbaked batter and bake for 40 to 42 minutes. (You cannot test for doneness with cake tester because cake will appear sticky even when it is done.) The icing sinks into bottom as it bakes and forms white ribbon inside.

Death by Chocolate
What a way to go!

2 cups flour
2 cups sugar
½ cup (1 stick) butter
½ cup shortening
4 tablespoons cocoa
1 cup water
½ cup buttermilk
2 eggs
1 teaspoon baking soda
1 teaspoon cinnamon
1 teaspoon vanilla

Icing:

½ cup (1 stick) butter, melted
4 tablespoons cocoa
6 tablespoons milk
1 (16 ounce) box powdered sugar
1 teaspoon vanilla
1 cup chopped pecans

Preheat oven to 375°. Combine flour and sugar in large mixing bowl.

In saucepan, combine butter, shortening, cocoa and water and bring to a boil. Pour mixture into flour-sugar mixture and beat. Add buttermilk, eggs, baking soda, cinnamon and vanilla and beat well. Pour into sprayed baking dish and bake for 25 minutes.

To prepare icing, combine melted butter, cocoa, milk, powdered sugar and vanilla and mix well. Add pecans. Pour icing over hot cake. Serves 15.

Oreo Cookie Cake

1 (18 ounce) package white cake mix
1¼ cups water
⅓ cup oil
4 egg whites
1¼ cups coarsely crushed Oreo cookies

Icing:

4¼ cups powdered sugar
1 cup (2 sticks) butter, softened
1 cup shortening (not butter flavored)
1 teaspoon almond flavoring
¼ cup crushed Oreo cookies
¼ cup chopped pecans

Preheat oven to 350°. Spray 2 (8 or 9-inch) round cake pans. In large mixing bowl, combine cake mix, water, oil and egg whites and blend on low speed until moist. Beat for 2 minutes at high speed and gently fold in coarsely crushed cookies.

Pour batter into prepared pans and bake for 25 to 30 minutes or until toothpick inserted in center comes out clean. Cool for 10 minutes, remove from pan and let cool.

For icing, beat all ingredients except crushed cookie pieces and pecans. Frost first layer, place second layer on top and frost top and sides.

Sprinkle crushed Oreo cookies and pecans on top.

Chocolate Turtle Cake

1 (18 ounce) box German chocolate cake mix
½ cup (1 stick) butter, softened
1½ cups water
½ cup oil
1 (14 ounce) can sweetened, condensed milk, divided
1 (1 pound) bag caramels
1 cup chopped pecans

Icing:

½ cup (1 stick) butter
3 tablespoons cocoa
6 tablespoons evaporated milk
1 (16 ounce) box powdered sugar
1 teaspoon vanilla

Preheat oven to 350°. Combine cake mix, butter, water, oil and half condensed milk. Pour half batter into sprayed 9 x 13-inch pan and bake for 20 minutes.

Melt caramels and blend with remaining condensed milk. Spread evenly over baked cake layer and sprinkle with pecans. Cover with remaining batter and bake an additional 20 to 25 minutes.

For icing, melt butter in saucepan and mix in cocoa and milk. Add powdered sugar and vanilla to mixture and blend well. Spread over cake. Serves 24.

Peanut Butter Pound Cake

1 cup (2 sticks) butter
2 cups sugar
1 cup packed light brown sugar
½ cup creamy peanut butter
5 eggs
1 tablespoon vanilla
3 cups flour
½ teaspoon baking powder
½ teaspoon baking soda
½ teaspoon salt
1 cup whipping cream

Icing:

¼ cup (½ stick) butter, softened
3 to 4 tablespoons milk
⅓ cup creamy or chunky peanut butter
1 (16 ounce) box powdered sugar

Preheat oven to 350°. Cream butter, sugars and peanut
butter and beat until fluffy. Add eggs one at a time and
beat well after each addition. Add vanilla and blend. Sift
dry ingredients and add alternately with whipping cream.

Pour mixture into large, sprayed tube pan and bake for
1 hour, 10 minutes. Test with toothpick to make sure cake
is done.

To make icing, combine all ingredients and beat until
smooth. Frost cake.

Yummy Orange Rolls

3¼ cups vanilla wafer crumbs
1 (16 ounce) box powdered sugar
2 cups chopped pecans
1 (16 ounce) can frozen orange juice concentrate, thawed
½ cup (1 stick) butter, melted
1 cup flaked coconut

Combine vanilla wafer crumbs, powdered sugar and pecans and mix well. Stir in orange juice and butter. Shape into 2-inch fingers, roll in coconut and chill.

Lemon-Angel Bars

1 (1 pound) package 1-step angel food cake mix
1 (21 ounce) can lemon pie filling
⅓ cup (⅔ stick) butter, softened
2 cups powdered sugar
2 tablespoons lemon juice

Preheat oven to 350°. Combine cake mix and lemon pie filling in bowl and stir to mix well. Pour into sprayed 9 x 13-inch baking pan and bake for 20 minutes or until done.

Just before cake is done, combine butter, powdered sugar and lemon juice and spread over hot layer. Cake will sink down a little in middle, so make sure icing is on edges of cake as well as in middle.

When cool, cut into 18 to 24 bars and store in refrigerator. Bars can be served at temperature or cold.

Macadamia Nut Cookies

½ cup shortening
½ cup (1 stick) butter, softened
2½ cups flour
1 cup packed brown sugar
½ cup sugar
2 eggs
1 teaspoon vanilla
½ teaspoon butter flavoring
½ teaspoon baking soda
2 cups white chocolate chips
1 (3 ounce) jar Macadamia nuts, chopped

Preheat oven to 350°. In mixing bowl, beat shortening and butter. Add half flour and mix well. Add sugars, eggs, vanilla, butter flavoring and baking soda.

Beat until mixture combines well. Add remaining flour, mix well and stir in chocolate chips and nuts.

Drop dough by teaspoonfuls on baking sheet and bake for 8 minutes.

Snappy Oat Treats

3 cups quick-rolled oats
1 cup chocolate chips
½ cup flaked coconut
½ cup chopped pecans
2 cups sugar
¾ cup (1½ sticks) butter
½ cup evaporated milk

Combine oats, chocolate chips, coconut and pecans in large bowl. In saucepan, boil sugar, butter and milk for 1 to 2 minutes and stir constantly.

(Continued on next page.)

(Continued)

Pour hot mixture over oat-chocolate mixture in bowl and stir until chocolate chips melt. Drop by teaspoonfuls on wax paper. Cool at room temperature and store in covered container.

Tip: Use white chocolate chips and ¾ cup candied, cut up cherries for a colorful variation.

Sierra Nuggets

1 cup (2 sticks) butter
1 cup packed brown sugar
1½ cups white sugar
1 tablespoon milk
2 teaspoons vanilla
2 eggs
1 cup crushed flake cereal
3 cups oatmeal
1½ cups flour
1¼ teaspoons baking soda
1 teaspoon salt
2 teaspoons cinnamon
¼ teaspoon nutmeg
⅛ teaspoon clove
½ cup flaked coconut
2 cups chocolate chips
1 cup walnuts or pecans

Preheat oven to 350°. In large mixing bowl, combine butter and sugars and beat until smooth and creamy. Beat in milk, vanilla and eggs. Stir in flake cereal and oatmeal.

Sift flour, baking soda, salt and seasonings and gradually add to mixture. Stir in coconut, chocolate chips and nuts.

Drop by teaspoonfuls on baking sheet and bake for 10 to 15 minutes.

White Chocolate-Almond Cookies

¾ cup firmly packed light brown sugar
½ cup sugar
½ cup (1 stick) butter, softened
½ cup shortening
1½ teaspoons vanilla
1 egg
1¾ cups plus 2 tablespoons flour
1 teaspoon baking soda
½ teaspoon salt
8 ounces white chocolate morsels
⅓ cup slivered almonds

Preheat oven to 350°. In large bowl, combine sugars, butter, shortening, vanilla and egg and mix well.

Stir in flour, baking soda and salt and blend well. Stir in white chocolate morsels and almonds and mix well. (Batter will be stiff.)

Drop by teaspoonfuls on baking sheet and bake for 10 minutes or until they are light, golden brown.

Store cookies in sealed container.

Butter-Pecan Turtle Bars

2 cups flour
1½ cups packed light brown sugar, divided
¾ cup (1½ sticks) butter, divided
⅔ cup (1⅓ sticks) butter
1½ cups lightly chopped pecans
4 squares semi-sweet chocolate

Preheat oven to 350°. In large mixing bowl, combine flour, ¾ cup brown sugar and ½ cup butter and blend until crumbly.

Pat down crust mixture evenly in sprayed 9 x 13-inch baking pan. Sprinkle pecans over unbaked crust and set aside.

In small saucepan, combine ¾ cup brown sugar and ⅔ cup (1⅓ sticks) butter. Cook over medium heat and stir constantly. Bring mixture to a boil for 1 minute and stir constantly.

Drizzle caramel sauce over pecans and crust and bake for 18 to 20 minutes or until caramel layer is bubbly. Remove from oven and cool.

In saucepan, melt chocolate squares and ¼ cup (½ stick) butter and stir until smooth. Pour over bars and spread around. Cool and cut into bars.

Hot, Icy Pineapple Squares

1½ cups sugar
2 cups flour
1½ teaspoons baking soda
½ teaspoon salt
1 (16 ounce) can crushed pineapple, with juice
2 eggs

Icing:

1½ cups sugar
½ cup (1 stick) butter
1 (5 ounce) can evaporated milk
1 cup chopped pecans
1 (3 ounce) can flaked coconut
1 teaspoon vanilla

Preheat oven to 350°. In mixing bowl, combine sugar, flour, baking soda, salt, pineapple and eggs and beat well. Pour into sprayed 9 x 13-inch pan and bake for 35 minutes.

Prepare icing as squares bake. Combine sugar, butter and evaporated milk in saucepan and boil for 4 minutes. Stir constantly.

Remove from heat and add pecans, coconut vanilla and spread over hot squares. Serves 12.

Carmelitas

Crust:

1 cup flour
¾ cup packed brown sugar
⅛ teaspoon salt
1 cup quick-cooking oats
½ teaspoon baking soda
¾ cup (1½ sticks) butter, melted

Filling:

1 (6 ounce) package chocolate chips
¾ cup chopped pecans
1 (12 ounce) jar caramel ice cream topping
3 tablespoons flour

Preheat oven to 350°. Using mixer, blend flour, brown sugar, salt, oats, baking soda and butter well enough to form crumbs. Pat down two-thirds crumb mixture into sprayed 9 x 13-inch baking pan and bake for 10 minutes.

To prepare filling, remove from oven and sprinkle with chocolate chips and pecans. Blend caramel topping with flour and spread over chips and pecans. Sprinkle with remaining crumb mixture and bake for 20 minutes or until golden brown. Chill for 2 hours before cutting into squares.

Buttery Walnut Squares

1 cup (2 sticks) butter, softened
1¾ cups packed brown sugar
1¾ cups flour

Topping:

1 cup packed brown sugar
4 eggs, lightly beaten
2 tablespoons flour
2 cups chopped walnuts
1 cup flaked coconut

Preheat oven to 350°. In bowl, combine butter and sugar
and beat until smooth and creamy. Add flour and mix well.
Pat mixture down evenly in sprayed 9 x 13-inch glass pan
and bake for 15 minutes.

For topping, combine sugar and eggs in medium bowl.
Add flour and mix well. Fold in walnuts and coconut and
pour over crust. Bake for 20 to 25 minutes or until set in
center. Cool in pan and cut into squares.

*Tip: Serve these delicious squares with a scoop of ice cream
for a great dessert.*

Terrific Almond-Coconut Squares

2 cups graham cracker crumbs
3 tablespoons brown sugar
½ cup (1 stick) butter, melted
1 (14 ounce) can sweetened, condensed milk
1 (7 ounce) package shredded coconut
1 teaspoon vanilla

Topping:

1 (6 ounce) package chocolate chips
1 (6 ounce) package butterscotch chips
4 tablespoons (½ stick) butter
6 tablespoons chunky peanut butter
½ cup slivered almonds

Preheat oven to 325°. Combine graham cracker crumbs, brown sugar and butter and mix well. Pat mixture evenly into sprayed 9 x 13-inch baking pan and bake for 10 minutes. Cool.

Combine condensed milk, coconut and vanilla and pour over baked crust and bake another 25 minutes. Cool.

For topping, melt all topping ingredients in double boiler and spread mixture over baked ingredients. Cool and cut into squares. Makes 3 dozen.

Icy Caramel-Apple Mousse

¾ cup (1½ sticks) butter
⅔ cup sugar
2½ teaspoons lemon juice
¼ cup water
½ teaspoon cinnamon
2 tablespoons rum
5 or 6 medium apples, peeled, thinly sliced
½ (16 ounce) carton whipped topping
¼ cup sugar
1 teaspoon vanilla
Peanut brittle, slightly crushed

Melt butter in large skillet and add sugar, lemon juice and water. Cook for 10 minutes or until sugar dissolves and syrup is slightly thick and golden. Remove from heat and add cinnamon, rum and apples.

Cook apples in syrup for 3 to 4 minutes or until they thoroughly coat and are soft. Remove apples from syrup and cool.

Add sugar to whipped topping and fold apples into whipped topping. Spoon mixture into parfait glasses or crystal sherbets and chill for several hours.

Sprinkle generously with crushed peanut brittle before serving.

Southern Pecan Bread Pudding with Bourbon Sauce

3 eggs
1½ cups sugar
2 tablespoons brown sugar
½ teaspoon nutmeg
2¾ cups whipping cream
¼ cup (½ stick) butter, melted
½ cup pecans
½ cup raisins
4 cups cubed, crust less Texas Toast

Bourbon Sauce:

½ cup sugar
3 tablespoons brown sugar
1 tablespoon flour
1 egg
2 tablespoons (¼ stick) butter, melted
1¼ cups whipping cream
¼ cup bourbon

Preheat oven to 375°. Combine 3 eggs, sugars, nutmeg, whipping cream, butter, pecans and raisins and mix well. Place bread in 6 x 10-inch loaf pan. Pour mixture over bread and bake covered for 20 minutes. Remove cover, cook another 30 minutes and cool.

To prepare sauce, whisk sugars, flour, egg, butter and whipping cream and pour into saucepan. Over medium heat, cook mixture and stir constantly, until mixture is thick. Add bourbon and mix well.

Slice bread pudding and serve with 2 to 3 tablespoons of bourbon sauce over top. Makes 8 servings.

Macadamia Island Candy

1 (20 ounce) package white almond bark
2 (3 ounce) jars honey-roasted macadamia nuts,
  chopped
¾ cup flaked coconut

In a double boiler, melt 12 squares white almond bark. As
soon as almond bark melts, pour in nuts and coconut and
stir well.

Place wax paper on baking sheet, pour candy onto wax
paper and spread. Chill for 30 minutes to set. Break into
pieces to serve.

Tip: Roast your own nuts by placing them in a dry skillet
over low heat. Toast until slightly golden and set aside. If
you don't have a double boiler, add water to saucepan and
place white almond bark in it.

Super Date-Nut Loaf Candy

6 cups sugar
1 (12 ounce) can evaporated milk
½ cup white corn syrup
1 cup (2 sticks) butter
2 (8 ounce) boxes chopped dates
3 cups chopped pecans or English walnuts
1 tablespoon vanilla

In large saucepan, cook sugar, milk, corn syrup and butter
for 5 minutes or until it boils. Stir constantly with wooden
or plastic spoon so mixture will not scorch. Add dates and
cook until it forms soft ball in cup of cold water. Remove
from heat and beat until thick. Add pecans and vanilla and
stir until very thick.

(Continued on next page.)

(Continued)

Spoon out mixture on wet cup towel to make roll. (Recipe makes 2 rolls of candy.) Keep wrapped until it is firm enough to slice.

Tropical Cheesecake

1¼ cups graham cracker crumbs
½ cup flaked coconut
½ cup chopped pecans
2 tablespoons light brown sugar
¼ cup (½ stick) butter, melted
2 (8 ounce) packages cream cheese, softened
1 (14 ounce) can sweetened, condensed milk
3 eggs
¼ cup frozen orange juice concentrate, thawed
1 teaspoon pineapple extract
1 (20 ounce) can pineapple pie filling, divided
1 cup sour cream

Preheat oven to 300°. Combine crumbs, coconut, pecans, brown sugar and butter and press firmly on bottom of 9-inch spring form pan and set aside.

In large mixing bowl, beat cream cheese until fluffy and gradually add condensed milk. Mix in eggs, juice concentrate and pineapple extract and mix well. Stir in 3⁄4 cup pineapple pie filling. Pour mixture into prepared spring form pan and bake for 1 hour or until center is set.

Spread sour cream over top and bake 5 minutes longer. Cool, spread remaining pineapple filling over cheesecake and chill.

Lemon Lush Cheesecake Squares

1¼ cups flour
⅔ cup (⅓ stick) butter
½ cup chopped pecans
1 cups powdered sugar
1 (8 ounce) package cream cheese, softened
1 (12 ounce) carton whipped topping, divided
2 (3.4 ounce) packages instant lemon pudding
1 tablespoon lemon juice
2¾ cups milk

Preheat oven to 375°. Combine flour, butter and pecans and pat down into 9 x 13-inch baking dish. Bake for 15 minutes.

Beat powdered sugar and cream cheese until fluffy and fold in 2 cups whipped topping. Spread mixture over nut crush.

Combine pudding, lemon juice and milk and beat. Spread over second layer.

Top with remaining whipped topping and chill. To serve, cut into squares.

Creamy Banana Pudding
Quick and easy!

1 (14 ounce) can sweetened, condensed milk
1½ cups cold water
1 (3.4 ounce) package instant vanilla pudding mix
1 (8 ounce) carton whipped topping
36 vanilla wafers
3 bananas

In large bowl, combine condensed milk and water. Add pudding mix and beat well. Chill for 5 minutes and fold in whipped topping.

Spoon 1 cup pudding mixture into 3-quart glass serving bowl. Top with wafers, bananas and pudding. Repeat layer process twice and end with pudding.

Cover, chill and keep chilled.

Fruit Fajita Rolls

1 (20 ounce) can prepared fruit pie filling
10 small or large flour tortillas
2 cups water
1½ cups sugar
¾ cup (1½ sticks) butter
1 teaspoon almond flavoring

Preheat oven to 350°. Divide fruit equally on tortillas, roll up and place in 9 x 13-inch baking dish. Combine water, sugar and butter in saucepan and bring to a boil.

Add almond flavoring and pour mixture over flour tortillas. Place in refrigerator and let soak 1 to 24 hours.

Bake for 20 to 25 minutes until brown and bubbly.

Oreo Sundae Favorite

½ cup (1 stick) butter
1 (19 ounce) package Oreo cookies, crushed
½ gallon vanilla ice cream, softened
2 (12 ounce) jars fudge sauce
1 (12 ounce) carton whipped topping
Maraschino cherries

Melt butter in 9 x 13-inch pan. Mix crushed Oreos (except for ½ cup to be used later for topping) with butter to form crust. Pour mixture in pan and press down.

Spread softened ice cream over crust and add layer of fudge sauce. Top with whipped topping and reserved crumbs. Garnish with cherries and freeze until ready to serve. Serves 12.

U.S. MEASUREMENT AND METRIC CONVERSION CHART

The following chart will make U.S. measurement conversions to metric quite simple.

1 teaspoon	5 ml	5 ml	1 teaspoon
2 teaspoons	10 ml	10 ml	2 teaspoons
1 tablespoon	15 ml	15 ml	1 tablespoon
2 tablespoons	30 ml	30 ml	2 tablespoons
1 cup	237 ml	237 ml	1 cup
2 cups (1 pint)	473 ml	473 ml	2 cups (1 pint)
3 cups	710 ml	710 ml	3 cups
4 cups (1 quart)	.95 liter	.95 liter	4 cups (1 quart)
4 quarts (1 gallon	3.8 liters	3.8 liters	4 quarts (1 gallon)
1 ounce	28 grams	28 grams	1 ounce
2 ounces	57 grams	57 grams	2 ounces
3 ounces	85 grams	85 grams	3 ounces
4 ounces	113 grams	113 grams	4 ounces
6 ounces	170 grams	170 grams	6 ounces
8 ounces	227 grams	227 grams	8 ounces
16 ounces (1 pound)	454 grams	454 grams	16 ounces (1 pound)
2.2 pounds	1 kilogram	1 kilogram	2.2 pounds

COOKBOOKS PUBLISHED BY COOKBOOK RESOURCES, LLC

The Ultimate Cooking With 4 Ingredients
Easy Cooking With 5 Ingredients
The Best of Cooking With 3 Ingredients
Easy Gourmet-Style Cooking With 5 Ingredients
Gourmet Cooking With 5 Ingredients
Healthy Cooking With 4 Ingredients
Diabetic Cooking With 4 Ingredients
Easy Dessert Cooking With 5 Ingredients
4-Ingredient Recipes And 30-Minute Meals
Easy Slow-Cooker Cookbook
Quick Fixes With Cake Mixes
Casseroles To The Rescue
Kitchen Keepsakes/More Kitchen Keepsakes
Old-Fashioned Cookies
Grandmother's Cookies
Mother's Recipes
Recipe Keepsakes
Cookie Dough Secrets
Gifts For The Cookie Jar
All New Gifts For The Cookie Jar
Muffins In A Jar
Brownies In A Jar
101 Brownies
Cookie Jar Magic
Quilters' Cooking Companion
Miss Sadie's Southern Cooking
Classic Tex-Mex and Texas Cooking
Classic Southwest Cooking
Classic Pennsylvania-Dutch Cooking
Classic New England Cooking
The Great Canadian Cookbook
The Best of Lone Star Legacy Cookbook
Lone Star Legacy
Lone Star Legacy II
Cookbook 25 Years
Pass The Plate
Authorized Texas Ranger Cookbook
Texas Longhorn Cookbook
Trophy Hunters' Guide To Cooking
Mealtimes and Memories
Holiday Recipes
Homecoming
Little Taste of Texas
Little Taste of Texas II
Texas Peppers
Southwest Sizzler
Southwest Ole
Class Treats
Leaving Home

cookbook
resources LLC
Bringing Family And Friends To The Table

To Order: **I Ain't on No Diet Cookbook**

Please send_____ hardcover copies @ $14.95 (U.S.) each $ _____

Texas residents add sales tax @ $1.20 each $ _____

Plus postage/handling @ $6.00 (1st copy) $ _____

$1.00 (each additional copy) $ _____

Check or Credit Card (Canada-credit card only) **Total** $ _____

Charge to: ❑ MasterCard or ❑ VISA

Account # _____

Expiration Date _____

Signature_____

Mail or Call:
Cookbook Resources
541 Doubletree Dr.
Highland Village, Texas 75077
Toll Free (866) 229-2665
(972) 317-6404 Fax

Name _____

Address_____

City_____State_____Zip_____

Telephone (Day)_____(Evening)_____

– –

To Order: **I Ain't on No Diet Cookbook**

Please send_____ hardcover copies @ $14.95 (U.S.) each $ _____

Texas residents add sales tax @ $1.20 each $ _____

Plus postage/handling @ $6.00 (1st copy) $ _____

$1.00 (each additional copy) $ _____

Check or Credit Card (Canada-credit card only) **Total** $ _____

Charge to: ❑ MasterCard or ❑ VISA

Account # _____

Expiration Date _____

Signature_____

Mail or Call:
Cookbook Resources
541 Doubletree Dr.
Highland Village, Texas 75077
Toll Free (866) 229-2665
(972) 317-6404 Fax

Name _____

Address_____

City_____State_____Zip_____

Telephone (Day)_____(Evening)_____